Break
Your Boundaries

A Helpful Guide to

Personal Mastery & Professional Excellence

ferryman
Learning Resources

Break Your Boundaries

A Helpful Guide to

Personal Mastery & Professional Excellence

Bharath Gopalan

ferryman
Learning Resources

Ferryman Learning Resources

Ferryman.co.in

Mail: FerrymanLR@gmail.com

Copyright © 2014 Bharath Gopalan

ISBN: Softcover   KDP- ISBN: 9781696318105

First published in 2014 by Notion Press, Chennai

Also by the Author: **SMART Presenter**

Contents

Encomia for the Book

I am pleased that Bharath has written this excellent book 'Break Your Boundaries', where he has chosen to analyze and offer valuable applications about quite a wide range of books, all of which focus on individual development. Instead of merely summarizing these books, it is refreshing to see Bharath treading a different path in his book - he has connected real life instances to his reading experience, thus providing great benefit to the reader. This is a wonderful book that should be read by anyone seeking to improve their personal and professional lives.

Professor Michael Marquardt,
George Washington University,
Author of *Leading with Questions*

Break Your Boundaries is a true, unbiased book on books, written from the heart and soul of the author who has spent countless years reading and researching the best publications in the self- help and personal-professional growth industries.

David Mezzapelle,
Author of *Contagious Optimism*
(Bestselling book series)

I am in absolute awe of how Bharath has lucidly assembled a rich compendium of 'personal excellence' books. What impressed me most is that while the collections form a remarkable sequence, moving on seamlessly from chapter to chapter, each of it can also be invaluably exclusive depending upon the reader's need and choice. Break Your Boundaries has the capacity to keep the readers in a captivating mode right through, resting on brilliant and easy-to-relate narratives of author's personal experiences. I hail the Curator in Bharath [the way he connotes to his role], in amassing the gems of an esoteric assortment beyond the normal confines, to a wider world of growth oriented individuals.

G.Udayakumar,
CEO, CoreMind

Encomia for the Author

I can recall the first time I met Bharath some seven years back. He was delivering a presentation as a prospective candidate to lead our 'learning and development'. He brought out candidly the learning imperative for business survival in his aptly-titled presentation 'Cementing a Learning culture for Building a Sustaining future'. Even before he ran us through the first three slides, I had made up my mind. Bharath has, ever since, been making an impact in every talk he delivers, every piece of writing he sends out and on every learner he comes across in his training sessions.

I am pleased to see that Bharath is coming out with his break-through book 'Break Your Boundaries' - an offspring of his obsessive pursuit of professional interests and his innate strengths of ideation and articulation. In his book, he has carefully laid out the vital steps that can pave way for professional success and fulfilment. I am sure this book will leave an indelible imprint on the mind of every reader.

A V Dharmakrishnan,
CEO, Ramco Cements

Break Your Boundaries is an outcome of Bharath's deep passion for learning and sharing. He readily connects with the learners of every kind and spares no effort to bring out their best for he believes that training is only a trigger to help one discover what is already in them, like apple-fall for Newton. He says training is all about designing apple-falls for people.

Narasimhan G, Founder, Bumblebee Academy &
Former VP, Oracle

This book is about what Bharath is naturally good at – bringing a book into every conversation; when you interact with him, he has an uncanny knack of taking you into a book that fits the context. What is even more appreciable about him is his cross cultural sensitivity. He can be at home anywhere.

Igor Altbauer, General Manager,
German Automotive MNC

GB shares his experience over the years through his personal anecdotes and brings live his teachable-point-of-view from some carefully chosen books. These books by themselves serve as a strong reference point in the areas of individual excellence and leadership development. GB's lucid presentation style makes it an interesting reading. I am sure career aspirants at various stages, be it an entry or mid level, or senior management, will find it relevant and I personally recommend this book to all career aspirants.

Sadagopan Viravalli,
Managing Director, Global Consulting Firm

An avid reader of Bharath's sort has got to be doing something that would benefit both budding professionals as well as those facing mid-career challenge. This I guess is the most cherished venture for Bharath to the extent I know him -an unstoppable thinker and a great human being.

Manoj Srivastava,
Dy. Director, AICTE

Right book from a right person... Bharath has broken boundaries not once but time and again. This book will be an asset for professionals and businessmen, as it is distilled from Bharath's rich experience and exposure blended with the knowledge he has acquired from reading hundreds of books and most importantly, from his ability to see things differently and get the best out of them.

Prashanth Kumar,
Motivational Speaker, Mysore

Foreword

Drawing from some of the influential books on Leadership offered to the world by legendary authors, Bharath has blended his discoveries and created a recipe, that gifts a range of possibilities

- to take control of your career,

- to know your purpose and develop your vision,

- to overcome obstacles,

- and most of all, to make the most of your opportunities.

GB has culled the essence, by adding his profound thoughts to vital leadership principles that have stood the test of time. This book stands out as a comprehensive guide to build successful and satisfying careers. Break Your Boundaries will inspire readers to excel in whatever path they choose.

- **Marshall Goldsmith**, author/ editor of 34 books including the global bestsellers *MOJO* and *What Got You Here Won't Get You There*; a **Thinkers 50** Top Ten Global Business Thinker and a top ranked executive coach.

*"There is nothing so sublime and pure
as knowledge (of the self) in this world"*

*"na hi jnanena sadrsam
pavitram iha vidyate"*

Bhagavad Gita – Chapter 4, verse 38

To my beloved father
who always peps me up with his immortal words:
"what matters is not what happens,
but how you react to what happens"

Opening Note

Welcome to the experience of books – some of the best books I have come across in the arena of personal and professional excellence.

There are books and books everywhere, but which book to pick is a challenge, particularly, if you are like me- crazy of books on personal excellence and leadership– these books belong to a different genre unlike the fictions that you read to entertain yourself or the text books that you read to get informed. When you read to improve yourself, you don't derive the benefit of the book unless you effect a change you intend to make. Though we may find most books inspiring, when it comes to implementing something from the book, we find ourselves losing the steam soon enough and we are back to our old selves.

In my struggle to put into practice what I read, one of the ways I found to be effective is sharing my thoughts with people in my life. Every time I share, I feel not only charged up, but my idea of implementing something gets strengthened. This sharing got extended to my training sessions and later to my writings and here they are - a few writings of mine about those books that had a deep impact in my way of being and thinking. I thought of putting those random pieces together and thus was born the **'Break Your Boundaries -** *Fresh Approach to Personal Excellence with 22 Books That'll Kick-start Change'*.

First, I should clarify what this book is NOT:

This book is not a collection of book summaries, nor is it a bunch of critical reviews about some books. No, it is not even a compilation of 'tips and techniques' or 'does and don'ts' culled out from the books. Nor it is a campaign, for I know how blasphemous it is to even nurture such a thought. These authors, whom I highly revere, command a mind-share of millions of readers world-wide that talking about their works can only help raise my stature as an author. And lastly, I must also say that it is not a eulogy of those books as well.

Then what is it about? What I am sharing here is just my experience of these books- how they touched me personally and in what situations of my life, they came in handy, what those few things are that I picked for myself from these influential books.

Before I give a quick glimpse how you will traverse the journey along with the thought leaders who will accompany us through their books, let me tell you my way of looking at the books on leadership and personal growth. There are books that help us with our strategies, skills and styles. I call them **'know-how'** books. The classic example is Dale Carnegie's *How to Win Friend and Influence People*. There are books that go beyond telling us how, but also help us re-discover ourselves - our innate talents and, strengths, deeper aspirations and passions, our values and principles. We can call them **'know-why'** books. And there are books that provide us the basic structures and systems that form the knowledge-base. They are **'know-what'** books. We usually have preference for such books that give us not only the 'know-how' but the 'know-why' too. You will also find the books dealt in here are predominantly of that kind.

Here is how it is going to go: you can see the theme of each chapter and the corresponding books that are connected with the theme:

1. Read For Results   : *How to Read a Book*
2. Be Who You Want To Be   : *First Things First,*
                              : *Start with Why*
                              : *Be Who You Want, Have What You Want*
3. Learn to Learn   -
4. Explore Your Talents   : *Now, Discover Your Strengths*
5. HeadStart Your Career   : *Outliers*
                              : *HeadStart Your Career* (My upcoming book)
6. Make Serendipity Happen   : *Flow*
7. Meaning Is What You Create : *Man's Search For Meaning*
                              The 7 Habits of Highly Effective People

CURATOR OR CREATOR?

'Why this book? Why are you riding piggy-back on the works of great authors? Can't you create something of your own?' a close friend of mine asked me when I shared the theme of this book. Yes, we need people who think new ideas and create new things. But don't we also need curators who will preserve the abundance of wisdom that has been passed on to us by great thinkers? Don't we need people who **share the best of their reading experiences which can benefit others?**

The curator of a museum is happy, not when a visitor appreciates his/her work, but when their curiosity is kindled by some cue in the museum to make them to go beyond the collection and explore further. For me, there is nothing more fulfilling than that and I am happy to play the curator of the museum of self-help knowledge. If I have not turned your curiosity to go beyond this book to the original works of the great authors, I admit that it is the failing on the part of curator.

I believe this book will just open you up to the new way of reading personal excellence books. My intention is to trigger you into picking the right books that are relevant in your context and delve deeper in to them to derive lasting benefits.

Happy reading!

Bharath Gopalan

1
Read for Results

'It is what we think we know already that often prevents us from learning'

- Claude Bernard

I have a problem. First, I didn't take the symptom seriously when my wife warned me that she wouldn't come with me for shopping anymore. Rather, it was a blessing in disguise though I pretended as if I was going to miss the great shopping experience with her. But later, when my daughter also joined her and pointed out to me bluntly that I was suffering from a mental syndrome of a new kind, I couldn't brush it aside anymore. Yes, it called for a bit of hard work at the beginning of treatment, but it has started working now.

Root Cause Analysis

Before I go into the treatment part, let me take you to the roots of the problem. I am not sure how it originated- whether it came from my genes or whether I acquired it as I grew. I remember both my grandfathers, paternal and maternal, used to be surrounded by books. While one would be immersed in Sanskrit scriptures, the other found delight with Edmund Burkes and Emile Zolas. At the same time, I can't ignore the early influence of my schooling also. I remember there was a selection from the book titled *'Self Help'* of Samuel Smiles- the lesson was 'Little Things'- as part of my English Prose in my eighth grade. May be, I could have caught the infection from my teacher Dorairaj, whom we fondly called as ABD sir. The way he dramatised this lesson for us - a particular paragraph on how an army was lost for want of a little nail in the shoe of a horse – is still fresh in my memory.

My first brush with self-help book happened much later during my college days, when my father, being concerned about my aloofness, got me the *How to Win Friends and Influence People*. But it worked to the contrary, for I got more confined to the book. After that, one of my cousins gifted a book 'How to Study' by Harry Maddox. 'How to Study' was soon encroaching on my studies. Later, as I got my job and moved to Bombay, I picked my first one on my own, very carefully lest I lavish my hard-earned money, from the only used-books vendor at that time in Sector-IX, Vashi. It was a 94-page book '*How to get rid of the emotions that give you pain in the neck*' by Merril Harmin. I burnt midnight electricity to complete not only reading it, but completing most of the exercises in it too. But at that point of time, I never imagined how big this addiction could grow, until my family diagnosed it a couple of months back and brought it to a halt.

Treatment

Nowadays I am better. I don't automatically get stopped on spotting a sprawl-of-books on footpaths nor walk into every bookshop I pass by and keep browsing the books endlessly, without any sense of time. Sometimes, it had so happened that the sales-men had to remind me with a polite harshness that I had to wind up as they were about to close the shop. What my daughter pointed out made lot of sense to me. She just said one thing that awoke me to my bibliomaniacal behaviour of buying and collecting all Coveys, Zigglars and Carnegies that I come across on my way.

She asked me to just do one thing and that worked: 'dad, why don't you put at least one thing into practice from the last book you had bought before buying the next?' Believe me! I have not bought a single book since then and now it is almost around four months. When I see the array of books in my bookshelf and those spread around all over in my room, they are not sitting quietly anymore, but each of them seem to be jumping out and asking me, 'have you started doing any of those things I told you?'

I am not alone

I just wanted to know if I was an odd man out or if there were others too having this dysfunction. I did a simple on-line survey among my professional network using the SurveyMonkey site and the responses were really consoling. First comforting thing is my friends out there were no different from me. Most of them were buying and reading books like crazy that helped improve themselves and they seemed to be least disturbed when they didn't implement anything from the book. But one thing that stuck the chord is that most of them were making an earnest effort to internalise the ideas of the book. Some of them even said that they didn't complete the books they bought but have no qualms about it. I felt the reason could be the cost-benefit analysis, since the cost invested is very meagre, there is no real concern even if no benefits accrue.

Implemented anything?

As to what specific efforts they have taken to implement the learning from the books, the responses were however, very diverse and wide-ranging. While Shivranji, a HR exec, says that she makes a conscious effort to put into action, Rajan, a training manager, feels that reading naturally gets internalised as he reads and it just flows when he gets into the situation. RN, who is in a leadership role in an IT firm, believes in a more systematic approach like noting down the major points and reading them through as first thing in the morning, whereas his professional peer GN feels that books can only serve to motivate, inspire and provide some tips and he says real personal transformations can come about only by real life experiences. Lakshmi, an architect, says she has implemented what the books had instructed, re-organised schedules, work patterns and diet habits. Sudanva, a cement technologist has tried to implement the learnings from these books, where as Natesan, a behavioural trainer, feels that books have not been of much help.

Do books help improvement?

Emboldened by the responses from the survey, I placed a question in a networking site 'What did you implement from the personal excellence book you read last?' The Personal Excellence books, or the PE books, are the self-help books in the behavioural improvement domain that help in enhancing one's personal and professional effectiveness.

One lady remarked that the PE books helped her reach the jar of cookies in the top shelf, by stacking them on a chair. My wife not only loved that reply, but further added that they helped in levelling the planks while preparing for *navrathri golu*[1]. But a more useful comment came from Judy Hojel, of Sydney, who remarked: I read self improvement books constantly and consciously, and try to implement two to three things from each book I read. I just finished reading a book called *The Power of Impossible Thinking* by Colin Crook and was reminded once again about how powerful our mental models are and how important it is to constantly check whether we are being imprisoned by them or believing something that doesn't even exist. Carolyn of Queensland University said: I have been able to turn my life around through my wide readings; my best piece of advice would be to just get started by putting one piece of advice into action and not to try to implement too many changes at once.

Sales-pitch or help-talk?

We have seen a huge boom in the PE books industry during the last two decades giving rise to the problem of plenty. When the options are abundant, analysis becomes complex and we tend to take the easier route rather than applying rigour of checking which books would really be of help in our specific context. It is also easier to acquire books than applying them in life. But how do the authors help the readers in picking the right books for them?

To take a more serious look into the problem, I went through several books to see what authors promised in their blurb or in the prologue and how they wanted their readers to read the book to realise what they promised. It appeared to me that many books do not want to put the things straight and say who they are meant for and what the readers need to do to get to where they promised to take them by the end of the book. Probably they kept their captions and prologues very generic with a marketing approach rather than attracting a specific target segment. Think how bizarre it would be, if the same thing happened with those dealing in specialised subjects like Physics. A book on 'Optics' may get captioned as 'The Wonderful Light' or a book on 'Quantum Physics' may get titled as 'Cosmic Beauty'. It is time we had some system to grade the

---

[1]Navratri Golu, is an array of shelves (arranged like the steps of a stair-case), for displaying the dolls and figurines of mainly Hindu deities during the festival of Navrathri(nine nights) celebrated in India during the month of September/ October.

PE books so that people at different stages of lives are able to pick the right kind of books. It also gives rise to the need for books of this kind that help readers in picking the right books for them.

Reap results from what you read

A book that sells a million copies definitely delivers a great result to its publisher and author. But are you getting your results?

When I was in school, I remember my mom preparing a meticulous list before she went for shopping, lest she missed out buying an essential item and more importantly to ensure that she didn't end up buying things that were not needed. Today, we are not doing it anymore, since everything is on display in the shop and we end up picking and filling our carts with whatever we feel like. But there could be quite a few of them, we may not use at all and consign them to our attics soon. This probably happens with the books too. Here are a few things that could help in making your reading render the results you desire:

Take stock: The good old way that works for procurement is to take stock. The stocktaking means making a realistic self assessment of 'where you are' and 'where do you want to go' in any specific area of self improvement. Then you can go about picking relevant books wherever the gap is a cause for concern and coming in the way of your progress. Or, you may choose an area of your life you want to improve in the course of next 3 to 6 months. The area could be career, health, finance, family relations, networking, confidence, communication etc. Be focused on what you want and while buying skim through the contents to see whether your specific need is addressed.

Personalise the book: As you read along, highlight the points you feel inspired about and jot down your notes and insights along the margins. This will provide you with continuity when you discontinue reading and resume after some days. Going through your comments and the highlighted texts can give you a quick snapshot of the book.

Share your progress with your PAL (partner @ learning): Having a friend with whom you can share your goals and commitments can help a good deal in your improvement. During my school days, one of my friends and I used a similar technique of exchanging five new words everyday to improve our vocabulary.

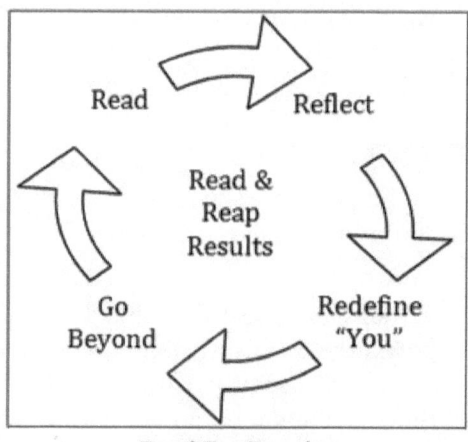

Read For Results

Have your personal excellence journal: Start maintaining a personal journal to record your progress with the new behaviour or habit and the break-downs you come across as you go along. Keep it self-motivating.

The Assumption Block

'This book is for readers who cannot read' is the first sentence of the book **'How to Read A Book'** by Dr Mortimer Adler, which was first published in the year 1940. It is a very bold and provocative statement to start. It can either put you off or provoke you to go further. If you take it as an insult to your reading ability you may stop reading. Instead, if it has stirred your curiosity, you will continue and you can really learn a lot about reading a book. 'How can I read this book, if I cannot read?' you may ask. The author makes the distinction by saying that 'mere knowing to read' does not mean one knows to read a book and he gives a very appealing analogy by asking: 'Do all the people who can hear sounds know how to listen to a symphony?' Many a times, it is our assumption that we know that stops the new learning. Nothing can be truer than the statement 'what blocks learning is what we think we know. It is a good way to keep questioning ourselves once in a way, 'do I really know or, am I assuming that I know?'

Though the title of the book is 'How to Read A Book', the author points out in the preface that the subject of the book is not 'how to read any book, but how to read a great book' and he goes on to give a 400 page treatise on reading a book. The book is interesting and generally applies to reading any book, but it is particularly useful in helping us read the all-time classics of great writers like Shakespeare and Milton, Aristotle and Plato, Galileo and Copernicus.

Implementation is the key

Adler brings out very strongly on the importance of practising what you read by quoting from Aaron Copland from his book on *What to Listen for in Music*: "If you want to understand music better, you can do nothing more important than listen to it. Nothing can possibly take the place of listening to music. Everything that I have to say in this book is said about an experience that you can only get outside this book. Therefore, you will probably be wasting your time in reading it unless you make a firm resolve to hear a great deal more music than you have in the past."

And there can be no better tip than just this one for reading any Personal Excellence book.

∽ઈઅઈઅ

Now, go beyond and read

How to Read a Book – *A Guide to Reading the Great Books*

By Mortimer J Adler

Thought Note

- How is your current reading aligned to your self-improvement goal?

- How do you want to capture the insights you get from your reading? Personalizing the book, Starting your journal, Sharing what you read with PAL

2
Be Who You Want To Be

"The two most important days in your life are the day you are born and the day you find out why."

- Mark Twain

I was excited, when got a mail from Walter Frick, Associate Editor of *Harvard Business Review*, saying "Thank you for your comments on the HBR article *Manage Your Work, Manage Your Life* by Prof Boris Groysberg on HBR.org. You're receiving this letter because we liked what you had to say - and we're considering publishing your thoughts in the **Interaction section** of the May print issue."

I waited for the print edition and swung into action as soon as I got the magazine HBR- May 2014. As is my wont of not losing even the least opportunity to tom-tom my brand, I scanned the printed piece and mass-mailed it to all my colleagues and close-ones. Below is the nugget of mine that found a place in HBR:

"What we need to strive for is to live fully, be it on the job or off the job, rather than trying to balance both. This work/life congruence can happen only when 'what we want to be,' that is our interests and values manifests itself in 'what we do'- our work. But in reality, what we do is more often determined by what we want to have, such as pay, perks or position."

But there was something more important for me in the whole episode. My pet-peeve 'work-life congruence' got its life back and I wanted to proclaim to the world that even HBR had acknowledged it. I pretty well knew that this theme was anathema to many to whom I forwarded the scanned clip - they have had several inconclusive arguments with me on this 'pay or passion?' theme. The fall-out was that I had to spend the next few days responding to the barrage of replies from them who, though were congratulatory of my accomplishment, more or less discarded my views as too Utopian and not practicable. They ranged from out-right rejection of the proposition to curious questions as to how one could pursue passion when one is already so entrenched in to the current career.

Let me share some of them here, for it is likely that some of the views could well match with yours as well:

- These are nice topics for books and talks; not for practical life;

- Though we realise that we need to do things we want to be doing, circumstances make us to compromise and do things for what we want to have.

- We only talk of success stories. But what about the sob stories of people who went broke pursuing their passion?

- When you get married and have a family, you need to plan for taking care of them rather than taking care of your own interests.

- When I chose my line of studies, I was hardly aware of the kind of job that I would land in; then where is the question of chasing my passion?

- Uncertainty / fear of future makes us stick to what we have got in, though passion could lie elsewhere.

- In today's world, hoping for the ideal situation matching 'what we want to be' may be a far cry. Instead, if we develop interest and strength in what we get, there will not be any dichotomy between life and work.

- Interest, strength and values are (mostly) acquired skills rather than in-born and better find it in the work you do.

- These are good probably for one who is in 'start-life' stage and not to people already in advanced stage of their career.

- How do those who follow their passion assess themselves against those who have achieved what they set out for, in terms of career growth, perks, position, assuming that passion-pursuers have not reached where they had originally set out to.

- Does it make your Work life balance more complete than mine?

- Blessed are those who do what they love and get paid for it too! Show me those people if you find them.

- In the current job market scenario, when one does not even get job in one's own field of study, where is the scope for fulfilling one's passion.

- How many are really aware of their own strengths, interests and values to anchor them into their career?

Of all the objections and concerns raised, I find the last in the above list very significant for, if that is addressed, the rest will get addressed as well. I come across people in their mid-career who feel stuck and want to make a shift to a different domain. They ask me 'what should I be doing? What career would you suggest for me?' They are clear about what they don't want to do anymore. But what stops them from moving ahead is their lack of clarity on what they want to do. The best person to answer this question is none other than the person who is asking. If we do not have an answer, we better find out and the earlier we did the better.

Your Career Shopping List

If you do not know where you want to go, how will you know what will take you there? But, we start working on how to get there, without even knowing where. Because the *where* is more often the place others are heading towards, rather than the one you want. If you want to tread your path, you need to heed to yourself and not flock with the herd.

The shopping analogy we talked earlier applies as well to career. Imagine walking into a shopping mall with a wallet full of money but without an inkling of what you want to buy. You may either end up buying a lot of things, which you may not need at all or you may not buy anything at all for you are not sure of what you need. This impulsive behaviour could be acceptable with shopping goods but not while shopping for your career. You can neither dump your career in your attic nor can you throw them out.

Obviously, no one would intend to do an impulsive shopping when it comes to much more serious matter like career and you would certainly have your shopping list for your next job, though you might not have perhaps jotted it down somewhere. So let's see how your list would run? What are the items you would include? Can you make a quick list of your expectations to make your next career move more effective? If you had mentally made note of a few items, then you will be finding the following in your list

+ Better pay and perks
+ Brand image of the Company
+ Job security
+ Designation or the position you would like to hold
+ More free time – less working hours
+ More autonomy
+ Nice-to-work-with boss and teammates
+ Less commuting time
+ Friendly work environment
+ Opportunity to learn
+ Future prospects of the company
+ Growth prospects
+ Opportunity for learning
+ ....
+ ....

Go on and the list until you feel you have exhausted of all that you want from the job. If you feel these are only very tentative items and there could be things you would have overlooked, then spend more time on preparing the list. Does it capture everything you'd want in your job? You are perhaps saying: 'why the heck this, when I am sure there is no job that can fully meet all of these?' But do you know the real reason why you don't want to engage in this inner process? Because, it is difficult- knowing what we want is much more difficult than getting it; we will have all reasons coming up within us to avoid working on it.

But, it is worth every effort for it can help you set the direction for your career search.

Organise your list

During my career coaching sessions, I ask the participants to draw a table with three columns and sort the items in their list by placing them into the column they belong: Be, Do or Have. Each of your career-wants could fall into one of the following:

1. What I want to Be?
2. What I want to Do?
3. What I want to Have?

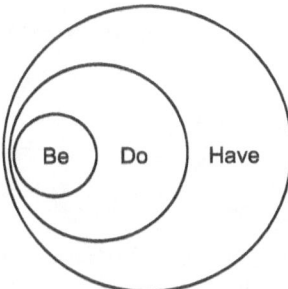

It is not uncommon if most items in your career-wants list belong to column 3 i.e. What I want to Have. Haves are tangibles that we can easily relate to, such as money, power, status, connections etc. You may have a few items in the column 2 - what I want to Do - which are about developing your knowledge and skills. How many are there in the category1- what I want to Be – which are about your strengths, innate talents, your values and principles. It tells you how much you expect your job to provide you the scope for being you – to live your values- what you stand for and to play out your strengths and talents.

Who You Want to Be: The Bigger Purpose

Is there anything wrong if your list is replete with 'Haves'? No, I don't say so. But, it is for you to see if you can have a fulfilling career if your 'haves' alone are met. In this outside-in approach, 'what you want to Have' drives 'what you Do' which in turn determines 'what you end up Being'. Inside-out focus is the other way round. You first try to find out who you want to Be - what interests you innately-what are you passionate about- what you stand for; when you have discovered your being, you start doing what you are passionate about to excel in it and eventually, what you want in your life gets achieved by itself. If not materially, it will certainly lead to a sense of purpose and fulfilment in life. It's worthwhile taking a few moments to introspect on who you are being right now and compare that to who you really want to be. Remember, knowing your 'why' - getting present to your purpose – is not a cakewalk; you need to be prepared to mull over the thought – keep pondering over it for long periods of time. What the books can, at best, provide is a structured approach that can help in this process.

Bigger the Why, Easier the How!

"When your *why* is clear, *how* is no big deal at all" says Krish, a psychologist and coach. He very succinctly brings it out in his blog:

A teenager asks 'How can I go to school when it is raining like this?' But he doesn't ask this question when he is on the way to his favorite movie. In one of my recent coaching conversations, this parent of an athlete (Olympic probable) asked me "How is it my son gets up at 4.30 AM to go to his sports practice, while I need to wake him up so many times to attend his engineering college?"

A young executive asks his Manager 'How can I complete the work, when the printer is not working?' He waits for the printer to be repaired. But, in the same situation, another person somehow finds a way to get it done. He does not wait for a miracle.

If we have a clear motive to get something done, we ensure it is done, irrespective of the constraints. This is the simplest interpretation of what Helen Keller had said of Vision: "The only thing worse than being blind is having a sight but no Vision"

The moment we have a larger Vision, 'work' becomes 'Mission'. For us, the biggest challenge is how to help our children, our teams and everybody around us to find a strong reason to live and work with enthusiasm. Even for this, we first need to get the 'WHY' as big and as intense as possible.

Start with Why

Simon Sinek in his book **'Start with Why'** says that every great company has at its purpose at the core which is what makes it great.

Sinek introduces his concept of Golden Circle, with *Why* at its core, *What* at the periphery and *How* between the two. Sinek asserts that the great companies and inspiring leaders think, act and communicate from inside-out, that is they discover their *Why* or their purpose for creating the company in the first place and then go on to their *How* and *What*.

Sinek gives examples of some great companies that communicate from inside-out, starting their message always with Why - their purpose, cause or belief, rather than with How or What they do. He exhorts: 'People don't buy What you do, they buy Why you do it.' It is Sam Walton's Why that gave WalMart to USA. Walton wanted to make quality goods affordable and available at the rural areas of USA. It is Herb Kellerman's desire to take the stodginess out of air travel, and bring it to the common people that resulted in SouthWest Airlines. Microsoft is the result of the Why of Bill Gates – his vision of providing accessible information for all. What drove these enterprises in the first place is the clear vision and purpose their founders had; making money was simply an incidental benefit of realizing their visions. The *Why* is the vision. The *Why* is the soul of an organization. It's driving power behind the company, and without it, you're just another corporate conglomerate.

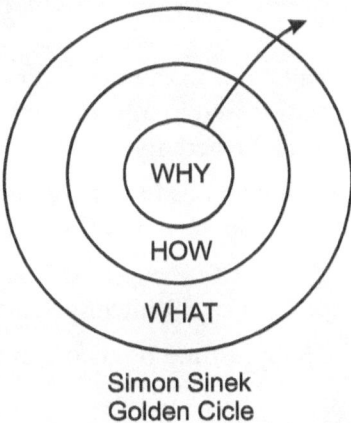

Simon Sinek
Golden Cicle

Whether you run a company or serve a company, you need to find your Why that inspires you and impels you to your purpose. Do you have a vision statement? Do you know your purpose for being? Spend a few minutes thinking about the *Why*. Your *Why* is deeply personal. Your *Why* is tied to a core belief.

Build Your Mission Statement

In the current style of living that we are entrenched, it is not an easy thing to get enlightened about our purpose instantly. We may need to take time by ourselves, probably for hours together at a stretch in an environment where we are unconstrained by time or the intrusions of our mobile gadgets. Best thing to do is to find a secluded place where you are totally alone and free from all interruptions.

What worked for me in building my mission was the book **First Things First** by Stephen Covey. I pulled out the Appendix Section (Mission Statement Workshop) of the Book where the author has provided a series of well-crafted questions that can trigger our thoughts in the direction of our life's purpose and mission. I took a sheaf of blank sheets and a pen, and set out to a secluded and serene place in the outskirts of the city. After I spent around four hours thinking and jotting down my responses, I felt I had got it and that was the start point for many things that followed in my life, including the book you are holding in your hand. You can try out and see if it works.

To get an idea of how the session would go, you may allow your mind to ponder over the following questions and listen to your heart for the answers:

- What do you enjoy doing the most? Recall an occasion when you got totally engrossed in to some activity that you lost track of time. What was the activity?

- Who is the person who has had the greatest positive impact in your life? What is it about him or her that you felt the positive impact?

- What are the qualities of character you admire in other people?

- What were the happiest moments of your life? Why were they happy?

- If you had no constraint of money and time what would you choose to do?

- What do you stand for? What are those three things that you value the most in your life?

- What are the achievements in your life that gives you a sense of fulfillment?

- What are you naturally talented in? How are you using your talents now?

- How satisfied are you with the current level of fulfillment in different areas of personal and professional life?

Another book that helped me a great deal in living my passion and constantly being reminded to remain there is the one my daughter got me: *'Be Who You Want, Have What You Want'* by Chris Prentiss. Practicing the exercises given the book is like meditation and can be life-changing. If you are prepared to put in more rigour in to this work of finding out your passion and making it a lively part of everyday living, this will be of definite help. It might take a life to complete the book, because the exercises given in the book are not something you complete once and forget, but live them all along all your life.

If you are getting into a frame of mind closer to discovering your 'why', it is time you worked on it further and get it out of your heart.

৵ঌ৵ঌ৵ঌ

Now, go beyond and read

Start With Why – *How Great Leaders Inspire Everyone To Take Action.*
By Simon Sinek

First Things First
By Stephan R Covey et al

Be Who You Want, Have What You Want– *Change Your Thinking; Have What You Want.*
By Chris Prentiss

Thought Note

Getting your 'Why' or the bigger purpose cannot be instantaneous. It is an inward journey and any journey can start only when you take the first step.

As you read this chapter, whatever initial thoughts you get could be that vital first step. So keep asking yourself, 'What keeps you going? What is the bigger purpose?' And jot down those thoughts here:

3
Learn To Learn

The only person who is educated is the one who has
learned how to learn ...and change.

- Carl Rogers

May 1986: I was excited about the job offer from the department of atomic energy. Apart from being a government job, what was more exciting was that I was going to work for one of the prestigious nuclear research projects and would have an opportunity to work with some of the best scientists in the field. I had a month's time to join the research centre at Bombay or Mumbai as it is known now. I was living in a small town in South India. Because I had a month's time, I wanted to go fully prepared for the job. I dusted out all the text books I had on nuclear physics and brushed my subject knowledge, and additionally borrowed books from library to equip myself as much as possible. I really wanted to impress my boss, whoever he or she was going to be, right from the day-one.

The Jolt

The D-day arrived. I was there at the research centre- centre was an understatement- it was a very huge complex sprawling over hundreds of acres with a lot of greenery around, surrounded by hills on one side and the Arabian sea on the other, both providing a natural boundary.

I reported at the huge engineering laboratory, where the pilot plant of the isotope separation project was housed. After the security checks, I was allocated a special pass to enter the control room, where I met, for the first time, my would-be boss for the next four years, a senior scientist, very down-to-earth person and the person whom I admire to this day for his scientific quest and personal humility.

I thought I would have an opportunity to show-case my preparation in nuclear physics. After a brief introduction, the first question Mr Gantayet posed to me was, 'do you know to speak Hindi?' I was jolted for a moment. At that time, Hindi was literally Greek-and-Latin to me. Leave alone speaking, I wouldn't even understand a syllable in Hindi. But he was not surprised, for he knew that I was from deep-South, where Hindi was neither spoken nor taught. Seeing my shocked state, he immediately comforted me -explaining me as to why it was important (as most people would speak mostly Hindi)- and asked me to take two to three months time to familiarise myself with spoken Hindi. And the best way, he said, to learn a language was to start using it without bothering about what others would think. 'You don't have to wait to perfect it before trying it; only by trying, you would get to perfection.' The rest was simple, for that matter, it took less than a month, for me to start speaking my butler-Hindi and in less than three months I was at home with Hindi.

Moment of Awareness

That jolt was important to push me to a new learning- that jolt was the point of awareness of my blindspot– that is, when I moved from "I don't know what I don't know (dk-dk)" to "I know what I don't know (k-dk)" state. When faced with a situation when my existing skills are not enough to cope with, I am pushed to the point of disturbance and learn new skills to survive the situation. This 'moment of truth' is the real awareness. If you don't know swimming and one fine day, you find yourself in neck-deep water, this awareness happens. In my case, it was my ignorance of Hindi.

When it comes to behavioural learning, a jolting feedback or some highly embarrassing event can create this awareness. For instance, some feedback on one's bad-breathe or body odour could change the oral hygiene and cleanliness of a person. However, general tendency is to block this awareness by getting into different modes of defence rather than confronting the truth.

Four Stages

I am reminded of a good old saying (not sure of the origin), which labels people based on the awareness of abilities and advises on how to deal with them.

"He who knows not, and knows not that he knows not, is a fool. Shun him.

He who knows not, and knows that he knows not is simple. Teach him.

He who knows, and knows not that he knows, is asleep. Wake him.

He who knows, and knows that he knows is wise. Follow him."

If you take only the first part of each line without heeding to the advice part, it tells us something about the stages we go through from being a fool to becoming wise. I will now paraphrase the saying into the four stages of learning we go through.

Stage 1: I don't even know that I don't know- I am stuck – let's call it *dk-dk* stage

Stage 2: I know that I don't know- I am aware – this is *k-dk*

Stage 3: I know that I know – I am conscious of my knowledge- I am learning – this is *k-k*

Stage 4: I don't know that I know – I am unconsciously doing- I have internalised my learning. Now, I am in *dk-k* stage

Learning to Unlearn

Let us get to some concrete examples. Have you noticed a stray dog crossing a traffic-ridden road? How did it learn the knack? Sheer survival instinct. But the problem with this kind of unconscious learning is that it continues to be in force even after the learning loses its validity. That is to say, we hold on to what we have learnt, even after the situations that caused the learning in the first place, have changed. If you pick the same clever dog that can dodge the traffic in Chennai traffic and put it in Stockholm, it will be terribly confused by the new traffic norms (with right side driving instead of left) and will kill itself on the road, unless it adapts its old skill.

Similarly, when we are pushed into a new situation, we desperately continue to apply our old skill, without realising that the old skill has no more relevance in the changed scenario. This calls for 'unlearning'. But what makes this unlearning difficult for us is the identity that we create for ourselves with our learning. If you remember, one of the important professions of yester-years was 'stenography' and when word processors and computers came into being and the executives started taking care of their written communication needs on their own, the stenographer became the Dodo. But many of them who stuck on with their label or identity as 'stenographers' refused to adapt and learn new skills and were rendered redundant.

Learning Cycle

This doesn't mean that we can be so simplistic about the situational demands of human learning. The external changes can sometimes be so swift and so diverse that it may demand radically different sets of skills at a rapid rate. Are we not seeing the rapid changes of skillsets-in-demand in the technology arena? When it comes to behavioural arena, the demands for new learning may not be very obvious. It is only by constantly looking around for cues and feedback, we can find out the need. Hence the essential first step is to 'become aware'. That is when we move from 'I don't know that I don't know' *dk-dk* stage to 'I know that I don't know' *k-dk* stage(see the box). This awareness of one's ignorance triggers the learning process. The rest of the things are self-explanatory. Once you feel the need to learn, you start learning and acquiring the new skill, knowledge, habit or behaviour that can help you survive and cope with the new situation. That is when you start going through the learning stage from 'I know that I don't know' *k-dk* to 'I know that I know' *k-k*. After you have learnt the new skill, you start practising it and by repeated practice, the new skill gets internalised and becomes part of you. At this stage, your skill is so internalised and natural for you that you are not even aware that you are using your skill or, you don't even know that you know it i.e. *dk-k* stage, or '**unconscious competence**', the term the trainers are fond of flaunting around. An often-cited example for *dk-k* state is driving. If you are adept at driving and have been driving your car through the same route to office every day, then over time, your habit of driving becomes so automated that you are not even conscious of your driving.

After going through the learning cycle, you may again find yourself at the beginning of a newer learning cycle. You need not always wait for an environmental cue or feedback to discover your potential flaws. Looking into yourself can also give this awareness. Education, it is said, is the progressive realisation of ignorance and I feel nothing can be truer.

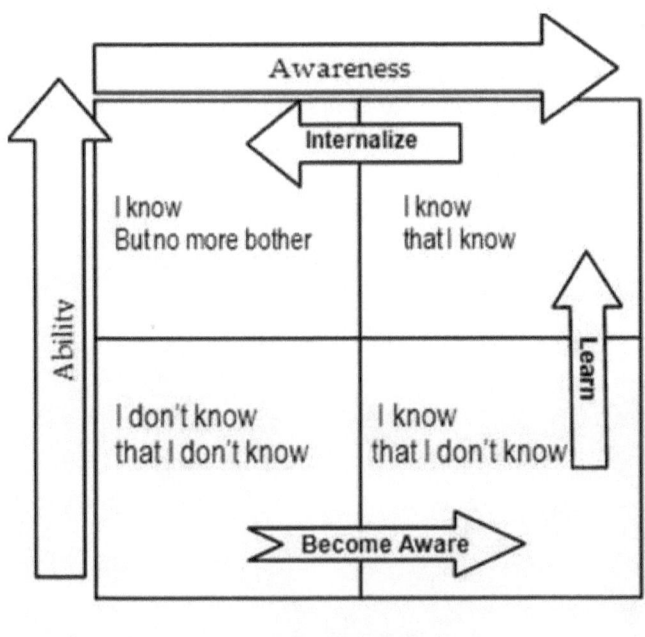

Learning Cycle

So keep journeying up the learning spiral and to find out if you are on learning track, keep asking yourself every now and then, what Emirates' ad asks: When was the last time you did something for the first time?

REFERENCE

The Learning Cycle above is adapted from the 'learning cycle' model in the book, **Total Quality Training** – *The Quality Culture and Quality Trainer* By Brian Thomas. I stumbled upon this in the Library of ATI, Mysore when I was undergoing training on 'Direct Trainer's Skills' in 1997. This model is being extensively used today by the community of androgogists, or Training Facilitators (to which I belong) and it is bounden on our part to acknowledge the source.

৵৵৵

Thought Note

There could be a jolt lurking around in the corner for any of us. The best way to pre-empt the jolts is to explore and construct scenarios of future so that you can prepare yourself in advance; for instance I could have started on Hindi even before going to Bombay, had I visualised the scenario, a bit more realistically.

Can you take a look at you crucial skills and explore as to what could be the new demands on your skills in future. How can you better prepare for such emerging demands?

4
Explore Your Talents

Try a thing you haven't done three times:
Once, to get over the fear of doing it.
Twice, to learn how to do it.
And a third time to figure out whether you like it or not.

- Virgil Thomson

Can a bathroom singer aspire to become a Latha Mangeshkar? Can a street cricketer ever hope to become a Sachin Tendulkar? What separates Formula1 racer from an ordinary driver?

'Quick-jump' learning

We will get to that question a little later. A page ago, we saw how we learn or how our circumstances force us to learn the essential lessons for survival. A shocking jolt that comes as a threat to our survival makes us aware of our blind-spot and put us on the need to learn or unlearn something. Over time, we become adept to an extent that survival is no more an issue; that is when we reach the point of saturation and there is no further learning. In my own case, I started learning Hindi language when I got a shock that my job could be at stake if I didn't. I went on and picked up the spoken language and I soon reached my saturation point when my Hindi was good enough to handle the day-to-day conversations. That is where we reach the stage of 'dk-k' stage or 'unconscious competence' (remember the driving example in last chapter?) where there is no further conscious learning. Nothing wrong with that since the learning itself started out of a weakness (ignorance of Hindi in my case) and not out of any burning desire to revel in the nuances of *shairy* (Hindi poetry) or to translate any literary work from Hindi. It was just to manage a weakness.

I term this type of learning as quick-jumps, since it is just jolt that throws you out of balance and you quickly get back balance after jump-starting to a new skill. Though the mental process one undergoes may be momentarily traumatic, there is quick pay-off when you take such quick jumps.

Let me explain it with a well-worn frog story. If you put a frog in boiling water, it would quickly jump out of the water. But if you put the same frog in cold water and slowly heat the water to its boiling point, it would not make any attempt to get out of water and it would boil itself to death. Don't ask me whether I had done this experiment. I have only heard it from someone who heard it from someone and so on. Nor do I know the psychology of frogs to tell you why frogs behave so. Frog stories are just good invention to say things indirectly, which if pointed out to us directly would hurt our ego and which incidentally, frogs will not complain about.

The point I want to make through this story is that it is easier to know when we need to get quick-jump learning, because we get strong cues or jolt (like being put into boiling water) about some weakness of ours that threatens our survival. But when it comes to building our latent talents into potential strengths, we hardly get any feedback from outside.

Inertia of action

We generally relate the term 'inertia' to 'lack of activity' or 'sluggishness'. But if you go back to your school, you will recall having come across this term, when your science teacher taught you Newton's laws of motion From what I mugged up then, 'every body (everybody?) continues to be in a state of rest or in a uniform motion' which is known as Inertia. Many of our day-to-day activities and routine habits and actions are akin to 'uniform motion' and hence qualify to be termed as inertia. All our abilities in the domain of 'unconscious competence', where we do not have to apply any conscious thought, are also just inertia in action.

'If you keep doing what you always did, you will only get what you always got' and if you are fine with what you are getting already, then you can afford to be in the state of inertia and continue doing the same.

'When was the last time you did something for the first time?" - an ad of Emirates Airlines used to throw this poser. Indeed, a very uncomfortable question, for those used to filling the days with routine stuff. Most of us (allow me to use this generalisation to rationalise myself) even tend to resist situations that offer opportunities for trying out new things. But query posed by the Emirates seemed to slap me on my face, "when was the last time you tried to learn something?" or put it bluntly, 'when did you stop learning?' If 'learning' were to mean 'mere reading books or acquiring more information', then we can blissfully say that we are continuing to learn. But real learning is something to do with 'doing something new' – doing something we haven't done before –doing something better. And if this something is not happening, then can we infer that learning is also not happening?

Comfort Trap

If you want to grow your skills into talents, you must have the ability to dig into them and see the latent potentials for improvement. Like said earlier, if things are learnt for survival, we reach the point of saturation at the point our skill is good enough to manage the situation and survival is no longer a threat. When people enter a new situation like joining a new job or shifting to a new profession, there is a lot of new demands from the situation like getting to know new people, learning the new tasks, understanding the systems and practices etc. There will be a steep learning in the beginning to cope with the demands. If the demands are too high to cope it can result in anxiety until the learning sets in. If the demands continue to be at higher level than the person's ability to learn new skills, the person may have a lot of stress and burnout.

As the person gets used to the new role and learns the skills, the demands posed by the external situations become too familiar for the person to handle and the person falls into the boredom zone, since there are not much conscious efforts required to handle the day-to-day affairs. The job becomes more like driving on the same road to the same place every day. We need to be cautious of this comfort trap, because this is the time, we may tend to become unaware of the slow boiling water that would one day become too hot to stay.

Incremental Learning

Let's come back to the question we started with: Can a bathroom singer aspire to become a Latha Mangeshkar? Can a street cricketer ever become a Sachin Tendulkar? Can you and I hope to become the super-best in an area of our choice?

Super talent was once a raw skill that didn't want to settle for mediocrity. But most of us build a skill to a level, our survival is not threatened and become comfortable with that. We may even be, obliviously, hanging on to our redundant skills, unless we are given a jolt of survival again. But instead of waiting for an outside jolt, if you keep giving that inside push everyday to move the boundaries of your comfort zone, you would have far travelled into a blue ocean, where competition becomes irrelevant. That is what mastery is about. Talent is just about unscrambling what is already latent in you.

When it comes to an area you are passionate about, your learning does not depend on external demands, but the internal push that you have for bettering it every moment. Your mind keeps going back to what you did and finds out areas you can improve and explores methods to learn the new thing. This constant inner push does not allow you to settle for what you have.

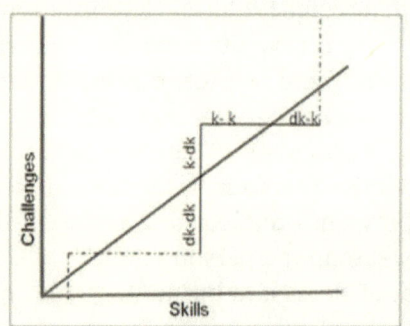 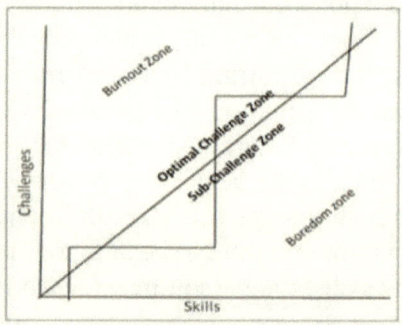

Learning cycle: from dk-dk to dk-k   **Zone of optimal challenge**

What makes the super-talented people different from the rest is that they, first, identified their strengths - the areas in which they had talents and were passionate about - and went about building on their strengths, while the others pursuing the same fields rested with far less that was just good enough. Obviously, the first thing is to find out what your innate talents are and then go about pursuing them. How do you pursue? You do it by constantly exploring your blind-spots or the 'don't know- don't know' aspects of your chosen field and learning and developing skills to internalise them in due course. That is, you will consciously keep yourself on the 'zone of optimal challenge' by putting newer demands on your skills everyday and going about fulfilling them. And hence, you never fall into a boredom saying, 'I am under-utilised' nor you are so stressed to brood that 'I am way too overloaded'.

When it comes to developing one's talent, it is more about internal push rather than external pull. You do it because you want to do it.

"Good is the enemy of great. And that is one of the key reasons why we have so little that becomes great. ... Few people attain great lives, in large part because it is just so easy to settle for a good life. The vast majority of companies never become great, precisely because the vast majority become quite good – and that is their main problem",

says Jim Collins in the opening lines of his book 'Good to Great'. If you really want to exploit your talent to its fullest potential, you need to be cautious of becoming complacent with becoming just good. So, you keep asking yourself everyday: What am I going to improve today? How can I do it? Who can help me? Have I become ok in this aspect and can I move on to the next?

Which Saw to Sharpen?

In a training session, I was emphasising on the importance of honing one's professional skills citing the good-old example of woodcutter's need to keep his saw sharpened to stay efficient. When we were discussing the analogy of 'sharpening the saw', one participant asked me, 'yes, I fully agree that we need to keep sharpening the saw. But the confusion is which saw to sharpen?' I fumbled for an immediate answer, because I knew that the right answer the organisation had was a wrong answer. What I mean is the conventional way used by the organisations to identify the areas for improvement (which saw to sharpen) comes from ones' weaknesses spotted by the boss.

'This fixation with weakness is deeply rooted in our education and upbringing' says, Marcus Buckingham in the book *Now, Discover Your Strengths*. How would you react, if you were a parent of a child who scrapes through in Maths exam with bare-minimum passing marks and scores a Distinction in Social Studies? Would you appreciate the child for the distinction in social studies, or focus on the poor score in Maths? Where would you want your child to concentrate more? The usual tendency of a parent is to do all that is possible to make the child to score better in Maths. The book cites a similar study which found that whopping 77 percent of parents chose to focus on poor score and only 7% of parents chose to discuss the subjects in which the child has scored distinction grade. This weakness orientation continues in professional life too, where the individual's developmental needs are predominantly identified from one's weaknesses.

So what is the right answer? How do you identify which saw to sharpen?

Discover Your Strengths

'The real tragedy of life is not that each of us doesn't have enough 'strengths'. It's that we fail to use the ones we have,' affirm the authors Marcus Buckingham and Donald Clifton in their book *Now, Discover Your Strengths*. They define strength as 'consistent near perfect performance in any activity.' The book reveals the three most important principles of living a strong life: **one:** you derive some intrinsic satisfaction from the activity which is your strength and you are able to perform consistently in that activity; **two:** you don't have to have strength in every aspect of your role to excel; and **three:** you will excel by maximising your strengths, never by fixing your weaknesses.

'You will excel only by maximising your strengths, never by fixing your weaknesses' says the book and goes on to offer some doable help to 'capitalise on your strengths and manage around your weaknesses'. Distilled out of a systematic study of excellence conducted by the Gallup Organisation over thirty years covering over two million people in diverse professions, the authors have extracted *thirty four patterns or 'themes' of human talent,* as they put it. These thirty four themes of talent form the basis for strengths. According to them, you draw your Strengths from three components, namely, talents, knowledge and skills. Talents are innate to you and are your naturally occurring patterns of thought, feeling or behaviour. Skills and knowledge can be acquired through learning and practice. While learning a skill can help you perform better, it will not take you to glory unless you have an underlying talent that supports the skill. Hence, the key to building a bona-fide strength, according to the authors, is to identify your dominant talents and then acquire the knowledge and skills in a focused way to turn them into real strengths.

What Changed For Me

When I was reading this book some six years ago, I was so eager to find out what my dominant talents were. Hence, I took the authors' suggestion seriously and went to the StrengthsFinder Profile on the internet immediately after reading chapter 3. I logged in using the code given at the end of the book and responded to the questionnaire at one go. The moment I completed the Profile, my signature themes, the top five dominant themes of talent, popped on the screen: Ideation, Strategic, Input, Learner and Connectedness.

Though all the thirty four themes are elaborately explained with real-life examples in chapter-4, my interest was confined to my signature themes. Certain insights offered by the book were so helpful that I started taking action on them. As pointed out by the authors, I could realise my lack of discipline coming in the way of leveraging on my signature theme- Input and too much of analytical approach blocking the effective exploitation of my dominant talents – Ideation and Connectedness. Though I was writing articles for magazines once in a way, I thought I didn't have it in me to write a book. Discovering my signature themes not only gave me confidence, but also opened me to the ways of leveraging on them.

It is not enough you identify your signature themes of talents, but you need to work on strategies and follow it with rigour in translating them into Strengths and harness them fully. And when you do that, you will not only find yourself on the path to glory, but you will find your life more meaningful and fulfilling.

Now, go beyond and read

Now, Discover Your Strengths – *How to Develop Your Talents and Those of the People You Manage.*

By Marcus Buckingham and Donald O. Clifton

Thought Note

Talent is just lying jumbled in the word 'latent'. Explore those innate talents lying latent in you.

What are you naturally good at? What are those talents you want to build on? What are those specific knowledge and skills that can help you leverage on your talents?

5
Venture on a Head-start Career

"You are now at a crossroads. This is your opportunity to
make the most important decision you will ever make.
Forget your past. Who are you now? Who have you decided
you really are now? Don't think about who you have been.
Who are you now? Who have you decided to become?
Make this decision consciously. Make it carefully.
Make it powerfully."

- Anthony Robbins

Dream Job Turns Sour

'It's very hectic. Surely, this is not what I wanted'.

'But weren't you so happy when you got the campus-placement?'

'Of course I was. It is one of the top IT biggies and the package was surely great. Who wouldn't be happy?'

'You got what you asked for. Why do you crib now?'

'But I never knew that I would be slogging my life out here.'

'You asked for it. Didn't you?

'I didn't have no clue.'

'Who do you think is responsible?'

'Why do you blame it on me alone?'

'Who else then?'

'The hiring crew from the company should have made it clear what the job is about.'

'Didn't they tell you about the job? Didn't you go through the job profile they had posted?'

'It was all gibberish then. I couldn't make much sense of it.'

'Was it their mistake? The company got what they looked for, for the price they could pay. What is wrong with that process?'

'You mean I am a commodity that can be bought and used the way they want.'

'Sorry if that hurts you. Tell me if you had said 'no', would they still be insisted on hiring you?'

'Probably no, because there were many takers.'

'So can I say you were interested? You passed their selection tests and interview, which means you had the right aptitude. For them you were just one of the Right-Fits.'

'At least, our college should have helped us in making a right choice.'

'Didn't they? They brought companies to your campus. They tried to ensure everyone got placed. Right?'

'All they were interested in was 100% placement. The placement team also hyped every job offer as 'Dream offer' and excluded us from sitting for the placement of other companies that came later. Probably, I could have got a better one later, had I waited. But I don't know.'

'All the dream you had was just getting into one of the top companies that walked into your campus. And they fulfilled your dream.'

'Agreed, my top priority was getting placed then. 'getting left out of placement' was really nightmarish for us.'

'So, this is what you have chosen. Right?'

'Yeah, at that point of time, but not anymore.'

'At least now, are you sure of what you want, so that you can work on your real dream offer.'

'I am pretty sure of what I don't want. But not really sure of what my dream job could be.'

'You are using the same model again, you always know what you don't want without knowing what you want, but the trick is knowing what you want.'

'I don't quite get it?'

'When you were in campus, you were sure of what you did not want: missing placement in top companies; but you were not sure of what you wanted: the kind of work you would like. Is it not similar to your choice of education: You didn't want to miss admission in the best college for the most sought after course? But you were not sure of what course you really were interested in."

"I agree, same is the case even now.'

'Are you ready to work on what you want?'

'I wish I had done it when I was in campus.'

'Better late than never.'

'Yeah, let us go'.

Dream offer or Dud offer

Why did the dream offer turn sour? Obvious, at the time of vying for placement job, all that was visible was the dream of getting a job in a big company, peer pressure and parents' anxiety arising out of 'not getting placed', imminent month-on-month cash flow etc. What were not seen: the long hours of work, back-breaking desk-bound job, rigorous online tests to keep the job afloat, odd-hour client calls and meetings, the pressure of deadlines and so on.

A business magazine conducted a nation-wide survey covering ten major cities across India on employee satisfaction. A large percentage of respondents were professionally qualified young people in the age bracket of 22 to 28 with one to five years of work experience. As reported by the survey, the top three reasons stated by respondents for choosing their jobs were Employer Brand, Pay and perks and Position or Job-role. When the same survey tried to find out why employees quit their jobs, the top three reasons turned out to be 'role-talent mismatch' 'lack of recognition' and 'work stress'. Is it not surprising that reasons for quitting the job are poles apart from the reasons for choosing a job?

Way out? Be a Venture Careerist

When you are in early years of your career and have a potential to get employed, you can try hopping jobs for some initial years to find your right place. But this trial and error method is a very crude way to get you where you want to go. Even, if by accident-which is a remote possibility, you get the work of your passion, you would have by then lost the precious initial years- filled with zeal and zest to learn and perform- which can catapult you into great long term career.

If you want these precious initial years of career to yield returns in the long run, then you need to invest in it, rather than looking for immediate RoI (return on investment) on your academic investment. The moment you complete your degree, be it graduate or master degree, and come out of your campus, don't look for filling your wallet, but fill your time with the value of experience.

Have you heard of Venture Capitalists? VCs invest their money in start-ups which have a promise – which have high potential and can take on an exponential growth path. The proven businesses that can give assured and immediate returns with modest growth do not interest the VCs. Because they prefer growth over safety, risk over run-of-the-mill and more importantly innovation over proven-lines.

You can be a VC too, but in place of capital, what you have for investing is yourself –your career. To be a Venture Careerist, the capitals you will be investing in your career are:

- Your specialized domain knowledge to meet the functional needs
- Your curiosity to learn new skills
- Your commitment to excellence in your chosen area
- Your accountability to deliver results
- Your insatiable desire to surpass the standards of performance
- Your ability to work with people
- Your readiness to walk the extra mile and go beyond
- Your creativity to innovate new ways of doing things
- Your resilience to learn from failures and go forward
- Your keenness to understand the business and contribute to its growth

Just not money alone

I don't doubt that anyone joins the job just to earn money alone. We all get into our jobs to deliver our best and it is the intrinsic nature of the job that keeps us driven. But over time, the routine becomes monotonous and we lose all our steam and go into the motion of diurnal tasks.

We feel a sense of fulfilment in our job, when we like what we do in our job and have the ability to meet what the job demands. Job satisfaction is a result of your interests (What you like to do), your skills (what you are able to do) and your job demands (what you have to do). To the extent all these three are in sync determines how satisfied one will be in the job.

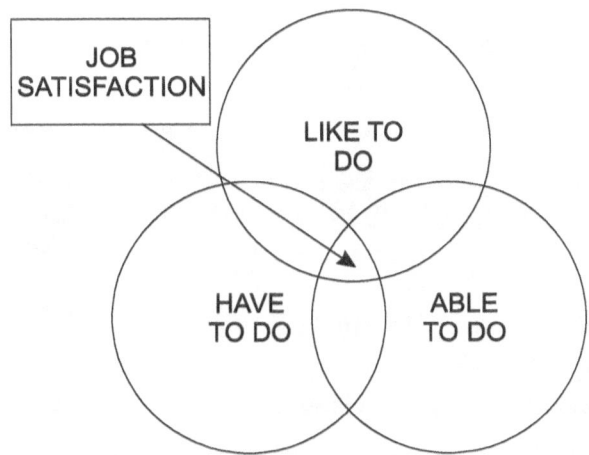

The eternal dilemma is whether to 'like what we get' or go chasing to 'get what we like'. More often, we choose to get our job first and then spend all our energy in trying to like what we get, until we get to the point where we are not able to take anymore. And we blame it on the lack of opportunities, over supplies in job market etc. Whatever is the reason we blame it on, we cannot leave our career destiny to be held hostage by external factors, for it is the place we spend most of our waking time and no amount of blaming it to outside factors will help in improving our work-life.

All it takes is some home-work to find out what our aspirations are and then align them to the realities of the job market. This systematic approach can lead you to a Head-start career.

Have a Head-start

Head-start means initial advantage in a competitive situation. A head-start is an advance position in start with respect to others in a competition, or which simply means, you are closer to the finish line or desired outcome. In competitive sports, such as a race, a head start refers to a start ahead of other competitors, allowing a shorter distance to the finish line. A head start could be an improved start in an attempt to achieve some goal, such as in one's education or the completion of a task. In such cases, the head start is usually earned by working harder or by using more efficient means of reaching that point.

A systematic approach to a Head-start career would involve the following five steps:

1. Discover Your Aspirations and identify the target roles you would like to take up

2. Explore the job market to find out the career options meeting your target roles

3. Empower yourself by arming yourself with requisite skills and knowledge and have a realistic plan to balance dream and realities

4. Pitch in yourself by building a right personal brand and be on the court- take action

5. Ascend the career journey

10,000 Hours to Mastery

What does it take to be the best in whatever you have taken up? Look at the people who have had very successful careers. There could be many factors behind their successes. But one common thread you will definitely see behind their success is the enormous amount of efforts and practice invested by them in learning, acquiring and mastering the skills that their careers call for.

Malcolm Gladwell, a renowned psychologist, calls it 10,000 hour rule in his book Outliers. He deduces that it takes about 10,000 hours of dedicated practice to truly master a skill, be it playing the violin, computer programming, or skateboarding. Gladwell studied the lives of extremely successful people to find out how they achieved success. He comes up with several examples of undisputable success stories, from the Beatles to Bill Gates, and very convincingly puts forth his theory that the biggest factor in their success is not innate talent or blind luck, but rather dedication to their chosen craft.

The Beatles played nearly 10 Kilo-hours together in Germany before emerging as "The Beatles" that took the world by storm, Tiger Woods put in his 10KHrs hours on the golf course before most of us can even drive a car with a permit, Bill Gates was geeking out alone on a PC putting in his 10KHrs as a school student at a time when many universities rarely had any computer terminal. In fact, closer analysis of success stories prove out that it is consistent and diligent clocking in at work in the chosen filed that plays a key role in achieving expert status in any field than any other possible reason.

It's a powerful message and if we are ready to put in that kind of time, then it is definitely possible for anyone of us to succeed in whatever we take up. Of course, connections, opportunities and luck can lubricate the path, but they can certainly not substitute for 10KHrs of work. 10KHrs of practice is the key to mastery and if you are prepared to invest that in the prime years of your career, you can be fairly sure of the imminent success.

Translating into Action

How do we leverage on this discovery uncovered by Gladwell's research? What implication does it have for us, who look at these achievers with awe and aspire to be there? What can we do about it? Is there anything that we can do to join their ranks?

The best we can do is to choose a field and put in a practice for 10KHrs. Let's do a simple arithmetic to check out how many hours of work you need to put in to clock 10KHrs in your chosen field of passion. If the time duration you are committed to invest N hours/ week in your chosen field, then it follows that the number of years you will require to attain the mastery will be equal to 10000/ (N x 52). Add this to your age to obtain the likely age at which you will be reckoned as an expert in your field.

Let us do a comparison of the number of years it would take to attain the expertise by putting in 10000 hours in the chosen field.

Case 1- you get your head-start job and you are prepared to put your best efforts of 12 hours of work every day on a 5-day week basis: $10000/60 \times 52 = 3.2$ years

Case-2- you get your head-start job and you want to have a relaxed work pace with 8 hours of work every day on a 5-day week basis: $10000/40 \times 52 = 5$ years (approximately)

Case-3- you compromise on a job to earn your living and want to pursue your passion off the job at your leisure and spend 2 hours per day (after work-hours) for 6 days a week: $10000/12 \times 52 = 16$ years (approx)

Have a Head-start

It just takes five years to achieve mastery in our chosen field, by merely working for forty hours a week. Many of us are already in a career for over five years now and have already logged in that 10KHrs of practice in some particular area. Then it is time we recognise that area in which we perform exceedingly well to be acknowledged by others as experts. But if we have not identified our passion area, probably we would have clocked in much more than 10000 hrs and yet we find ourselves not making much headway into it. And not everyone can expect to reap results out of long years of practice alone.

It is not mere clocking of 10 Khrs practice that can lead one to mastery, but what is more important in is to first identify one's field of practice by exploring one's innate talents and interests that have the best market potential and then putting in the discipline of 10000 hrs of practice. That is the way you can maximise your returns on the investment you make in your career.

If you are a career aspirant or still working on identifying your career-line, it is time you take a call: which one of the three cases would be your choice - to have a Head-start career pursue your passion on the job or, have patience with your passion and putting it off as leisure time activity?

Tap Your Talent Capital

If you're having your own business or heading a company, think of what your company does better than others? What is it that your employees or your team members do better than anybody? How do you create an environment that helps your people identify their talents and provide the opportunity for practice?

ख़ख़ख़

Now, go beyond and read

Outliers – *The Story of Success*

By Malcolm Gladwell

Also, look forward to an upcoming book (to be released shortly) by the author:

HeadStart Your Career

By Bharath Gopalan

Thought Note

Consider the next five years as the path to career mastery? Where, in which specific field, do you want to make your mark?

Are you committed to growing yourself in that field? What specific actions you can take today? How much time you are prepared to invest in it every day- day after day, every week- week after week, for the next five years?

6

Make Serendipity Happen

Take up one idea. Make that one idea your life - think
of it, dream of it, live on that idea. Let the brain, muscles,
nerves, every part of your body, be full of that idea, and
just leave every other idea alone. This is the way to success;
that is way great spiritual giants are produced.

- Swami Vivekananda

Being in Form

'Robin is unstoppable; he is in a 'form' of his lifetime,' extolled the commentator. It couldn't have been said any better to describe the way Robin was smashing every bowler; he was hooking every ball to the boundary line with ease - some landing in the stands amidst the noisy spectators, who were all cheers; no strategy - changing the bowler, re-arranging the field position – none seemed to work for the opponent team; Robin was going on with his demolition undeterred. The famous word for this state in the cricket world is 'form'.

The music composer comes to the sets, goes straight to his room without talking to anyone around and locks himself up. He sets himself in a meditative mood for about half an hour before he gets into the recording theatre. And once he takes his position in the recording theatre, he swings around his magic wand to create the melody out of the lyric that is handed to him. The music just flows.

"Music is something that should happen like a flowing river or waves of the sea. You cannot make it," says a legendary musician, who has composed music for more than one thousand songs in five different Indian languages.

Worshipper of Work

'We all have had our moments of form or being in 'zone'. We have experienced moments when we were fully engrossed into the task at hand without even conscious of the time that had flown by. I remember having studied a poem by name '*Karumame Kannayinaar*' (Worshipper of Work) in my native tongue. It translates something like this: 'they don't feel the physical pain; nor do they feel their hunger; they forget sleep; they can't think of any harm to anybody; they don't expect any praise; for the only focus of their eyes is their work.'

Flow

Psychologist Mihaly Csikszentmihalyi, who has extensively studied the phenomena of happiness defines 'flow' as "the state in which people are so involved in an activity that nothing else seems to matter" in his book titled '*Flow: The Psychology of Optimal Experience*'. He examines the process of achieving happiness and control over one's inner life in his book. He describes the mental state of flow as "being completely involved in an activity for its own sake. The ego falls away. Time flies. Every action, movement, and thought follows inevitably from the previous one, like playing jazz. Your whole being is involved, and you're using your skills to the utmost." He terms such a state in which the person experiences complete harmony of thoughts, emotions and all senses as 'autotelic' experience, derived from the Greek words, *auto* meaning self, *telos* meaning goal. That is, in 'flow' state, the goal of the activity is the activity itself and not the results or consequences of the activity. You can't get into 'form' in cricket if your eyes are on the scoreboard, rather than on the ball, nor can a musician 'flow' with the music, if his attention is in getting an applause from audience.

For those interested in the source, here is a transliteration of the Tamil poem from *Nidineri-vilakkam* written by Kumaraguruparar during the seventeenth century: *Mei varutham paaraar; Pasi nokkar; Kan thunjar; Evvevar teemaiyum merkolaar; Sevvi arumaiyum paaraar; Avamadippum kollar; Karumame kannayinaar.*

How do you know when you are in 'flow'? From the extensive studies Mihaly has carried out, he asserts that one would experience at least one, and often, all of the following conditions when one is in 'flow'. You can check if you experience the following to know whether you are in flow:

1. You get completely involved in what you are doing.

2. You feel a sense of ecstasy–of being outside of everyday reality.

3. There is a great sense of inner clarity–you know what needs to be done, and how well you are doing.

4. You are certain that the activity is doable and that you have the skills to carry out the task.

5. You experience a sense of serenity without any worries about yourself, and a feeling of growing beyond the boundaries of the ego.

6. You experience timelessness–thoroughly focused on the present, hours seems to pass by in minutes.

7. There is a deep intrinsic motivation–whatever produces flow becomes its own reward.

People can have Flow experiences in different ways. For some, flow may occur while engaging in sport activities such as running, playing a game of tennis or football; for some it could be a very personally engaging activity such as writing, painting, or sketching.

"Flow also happens when a person's skills are fully involved in overcoming a challenge that is just about manageable, so it acts as a magnet for learning new skills and increasing challenges," Csíkszentmihályi explains. "If challenges are too low, one gets back to flow by increasing them. If challenges are too great, one can return to the flow state by learning new skills."

Serendipity- a Lucky Accident or Magic of the Attentive Mind?

When I was reading this book 'Flow', I was flowing with the author's thoughts with ease. I could sense that I was in a state where at least five of the conditions of 'flow' were fulfilled. As I was wondering if 'reading' could be included as an activity where 'flow' can be experienced, a thought crossed my mind like a flash: Can 'serendipity' be attributed to state of 'flow'? I felt the random occurrence of the thought of 'serendipity' while flowing with the book 'flow' itself could be a case of serendipity.

First, we need take a look at the term 'serendipity' in this context. We may know 'serendipity' as "fortunate happenstance" or "pleasant surprise", and even the dictionary defines serendipity as 'the faculty of making happy and unexpected discoveries by accident', but we can get the real sense of the word only when we know how Horace Walpole, who originally coined the word, defined it. This is what Wikipedia says about the origin of the word 'serendipity': Walpole explained an unexpected discovery he had made by reference to a Persian fairy tale, *The Three Princes of Serendip*. The princes were "always making discoveries, by accidents and sagacity, of things which they were not in quest of". Incidentally, Serendip seems to have come from its Sanskrit root '*swarna dweepa*' or the island of gold.

Coming back to semantics of the term, it is not mere luck that can lead to serendipity, but also the ability of the individual to have the "sagacity" or wisdom to connect the seemingly accidental happening in order to come to a valuable conclusion.

Serendipity – Is it an Accidental 'Flow'?

To give you an example of serendipity, Percy Spencer, surprised by the melted candy in his trouser pocket when he was working near an operating radar, got curious about the incident and eventually his curiosity to probe further lead to the invention of microwave. But was it just a lucky accident? No, that would be too naive of us to think so. Not everyone who came across a similar experience would go on to invent microwave. It is only the attentive mind that sees the gravitation in the apple fall or the buoyancy in the bath tub. Beethoven composed his symphonies not by listening to the music but by listening to the silence within. I feel serendipity is the way the nature rewards the focused minds with the unexpected results.

What we need to keep in mind is that what we seek is always there around but it is for us to stay focused to find them. Have you not come across some accidental coincidences like bumping on a person whom you wanted to meet very badly for sometime, or coming across the song you were just humming? We consider these as petty incidences and discard them. But I feel this happens only when there is a momentary harmony of our mind with our environment. That is why, we are able to find that something that the mind is already in sync with. Though I don't have any empirical evidence, I am, somehow, conceptually convinced that 'serendipity' happens only when one is experiencing a state of 'flow' – the harmony of thoughts, emotions and actions.

Make Serendipity Happen For You

Every day we have a few hundreds of thoughts crossing our mind –it goes on non-stop, jumping from one to another, then to another and so on. If you google about this, you will be surprised to learn that it is not just few hundreds, but much larger: it is said that each of us think around fifty to sixty thousand thoughts during the waking hours of a single day. Willy-nilly, it goes on – this incessant thought phenomenon (can we call it ITP) in everyone of us.

What are we left with at the end of each day? How have we utilised this ITP engine that generates so much every day. The simple reason that we don't really harness the real power is because we don't exercise any conscious channelling of thoughts and they are just random, scattered and circumstantial, and are shifting according to the environmental demands.

But if we are able to focus to around five to ten percent of a day's thoughts, and orient them to a particular 'context', the concentration can probably lead us into a state of flow and eventually to the congruence of our consciousness with 'what we come across'. There is an old saying that says, *'the guru appears when you are prepared'*. The Sanskrit word *guru* (*gu* - darkness; *ru*- who or that which removes) does not necessarily mean a person, but anything, could even be an event, that removes darkness. There is light all around us, but it is only a prepared mind that sees the light. And when you are prepared, serendipity just happens.

৽৽৽

Now, go beyond and read

Flow – *The Psychology of Optimal Experience*
By Mihaly Csikszentmihalyi

Thought Note

Try it on a single day and see how it works.

As you wake up from your bed in the morning, take any single thought as your 'Context' for the day, e.g.: gratitude-'be-thankful', curiosity-'ask-why', appreciation- 'find-good-in-everything' or anything that appeals to you as your idea. Try to keep a conscious attention to the context of the day.

You are likely to stumble upon some serendipity or an accidental surprise. Even if not, you will be amazed at yourself- the power of your mind to create what it (you) wants.

7

Meaning is What You Create

*Your living is determined not so much by what life
brings to you as by the attitude you bring to life; not
so much by what happens to you as by the way your mind
looks at what happens.*

- Khalil Gibran

Prisoners of the Past

How did we become the way we are today? It is not that one fine day
we got up from our bed and found ourselves this way. Whatever we are
today is the sum-total of our past actions. As Sadguru Jaggi puts it in
his typically-humorous style, 'we are nothing but a heap of food and
impressions'. Everything we are today - our habits, behaviours, attitude,
fears- has its roots in our past. If you take a pause and probe in to
your past, you will be surprised to find how some trivial incident that
happened long back is still at the root of some fears and inhibitions that
you hold to this day. We don't even realise how a very petty and common
incident could rule the roost and play a disastrous role in one's life.

Let's me tell you a real-life story. The narrator could vividly recall
what happened and when. He was studying in seventh grade in an
English medium school. It was during a geography period, the teacher
was teaching about the contours and topography of India and how they

affected the direction of river flow. Half-way through the lesson, the teacher threw a general question: 'why do the rivers in south India flow from west to east and not the other way round?' The boy got excited, because he knew the answer. Quickly he raised his hand with all the gusto and he was so excited to see he was the only one in the entire class. He had thought up the answer in his mother tongue and before he could frame it up in English, teacher asked him to answer. Alas, the teacher would not brook the use of mother tongue in class. He fumbled and then managed to say, 'western ghats are taller than eastern ghats'. The teacher remarked in a funny tone, 'when did the rivers start mountain-jumping?' The whole class roared in laughter. And he was so ashamed he didn't talk at all for the whole day. Somewhere deep inside him, a decision got made- that raising hands is not done - don't take risks- don't speak unwarranted- don't volunteer -don't get into trouble. As he went about his life, he found ingenious ways to avoid any situation like seminars, meetings where he would need to make presentations, answer questions or deliver talks –without even being aware of why he had this unknown fear. It became a stumbling block for his professional growth. What a relief it was, when the awareness dawned upon him during an activity in a Landmark Forum session, where the participants were asked to look into the stories that ran their lives. Don't ask me how I knew his story. Who else would know it any better than the boy himself?

Automated Meanings

As we grow up, we become so adept at interpreting anything so instantly that our response becomes almost a reflex action. We combine and collapse 'what happened' with our 'story' or the interpretation of 'what happened' so fast and so automatically, that we don't realise it is only our story and not the fact. We become the typical Pavlovan dog taking the bell-ringing for the food. We are so conditioned that we automatically respond in a particular way to any particular stimulus. We become a reflection or reaction of innumerable stimuli that are thrown at us in the form of comments, opinions, perceptions, gestures and whatever we felt was directed at us: 'you must be a real dud that you can't understand such a simple thing'; 'you will never be good at maths'; 'you are useless' etc.

Though we cannot deny the effect of conditioning in our life – the fixed ways in which we respond to different stimuli, there is undeniable possibility that we can exercise control on the way we respond to them. We, human beings, are endowed with a unique ability – we have the freedom to choose our response, no matter what the stimulus is. This is what elevates the human beings from other living creatures. That is what provides human beings with limitless possibilities.

Show the Other Cheek

In this context, I can't forget a particular scene from the movie Gandhi, where Gandhi is shown walking along with Charlie Andrews and having a chat. Three white men are standing on their way with stones in their hands. Fearing they would attack, Charlie tells Gandhi that they turn back. Instead Gandhi diverts the topic and refers from Jesus' sayings, 'if a man slaps you on one cheek, show him the other cheek too' and asks Charlie what it meant. When Charlie says that it is not to be understood literally, it is metaphorical, Gandhi continues saying he guessed 'that Jesus meant one must show courage and be willing to take one blow or several blows, to demonstrate that you will not strike back nor run away. That calls on something in the enemy that makes his hatred for you decrease and his respect for you increase.'

Gandhi gives a powerful interpretation to the teaching of Lord Jesus. 'Showing the other cheek' means power to control our response to the stimulus: 'you can only give a slap; but you cannot give me pain for I am the one to decide that; by merely inflicting hurt, you cannot make me suffer, because I am the one to decide whether or not to suffer'. It applies not only to situations where someone behaves violently towards us, but to any adverse situation that we come across in our life. Our normal tendency is to instantly react to the situation emotionally out of fear or out of anger. If we are afraid, we might run away from the scene or if we feel strong and angry, we may put up a fight. But it calls for a lot of courage, composure and wisdom to respond peacefully without any emotional knee-jerk reactions. It calls for the very unique ability of human beings to use the very subtle power to respond to the stimulus in a way you want rather than reacting the way it wants you to react. That distinguishes between whether you are the master of your destiny or a creature of your environment.

Freedom to Choose one's Attitude

"Everything can be taken from a man but one thing: the last of human freedoms—to choose one's own attitude in any given set of circumstances—to choose one's own way", says Victor Frankl in his book *Man's Search for Meaning in Life*. Victor Frankl, a neurologist and psychiatrist, who underwent the harshest of treatments any human being can undergo, as a concentration camp inmate during the Second World War, writes about his experience in this book, which led to his discovery of 'logotherapy'. Having lost his father, brother, mother and his wife in the camps and being subjected to hunger, cold and brutality, how could he find his life worth preserving? How could he make sense of this apparently senseless suffering? What made his life worth living for even while suffering in such brutal conditions? It is where Frankl created a powerful meaning for his life and discovered how the 'the will to meaning' is an essential motivation for life. In the midst of the most painful, and dehumanizing situation, he was going through in the concentration camp, he discovers within himself the 'power to choose his response' to whatever was happening to him- whatever tortures he was being put through and that ability to respond is given by the purpose or meaning in his life. Frankl says that those who survived longest in concentration camps were not those who were physically strong, but those who retained a sense of purpose.

Mental well-being depends on a certain degree of tension between 'what one is' and 'what one should become' which gives a potential meaning waiting to be fulfilled by the person. The striving to find a meaning in one's life is the primary motivational force and this forms the basis for Frankl's logotherapy. The goal of logotherapy (derived from Greek 'logos' denoting 'meaning' or 'purpose') is to carry out an existential analysis of the person and, in so doing, to help him find the meaning for his life. According to Frankl, we can discover this meaning through:

- Creating a work or giving something to the world through self-expression,

- Experiencing the world by interacting authentically with our environment and with others, and

- Changing our attitude when we are faced with unavoidable suffering - situation or circumstance that we cannot change.

Proactivity is Response-ability

Taking cue from Frankl, Stephan Covey draws 'the habit of *proactivity*' as the first and most basic of '*The 7 Habits of Highly Effective People*' in his very famous book of the same title. Proactivity is much more than merely taking initiative; It is about taking responsibility to make things happen. Responsibility or response-ability is the ability to choose your response, irrespective of the circumstances - the stimuli from the environment. When you are reactive, you put the blame on the situation or on people or on anything that is outside you. You are just a bundle of automated reactions and you give the power to the reasons outside you to determine your actions. When you are responsible, you don't give in to the reasons and blame the circumstances, but you become the cause in the matter of making things happen. You move from 'because' to 'being the cause'. You do what you choose to do and become what you choose to become. That leaves you with immense power– with infinite possibilities.

ക‌ക‌ക

Now, go beyond and read

Man's Search for Meaning

By Viktor E Frankl

The 7 Habits of Highly Effective People -*Powerful Lessons in Personal Change*

By Stephen R Covey

Thought Note

Can you get present to the automated responses in your daily routine? (for instance: getting urge to have a cup of coffee at a particular time of the day)

Can you exercise your 'free' response without being impacted by the stimulus?

8

Master the Inner Talk

"We are responsible for what we are, and whatever we wish ourselves to be, we have the power to make ourselves. If what we are now has been the result of our own past actions, it certainly follows that whatever we wish to be in future can be produced by our present actions; so we have to know how to act."

- Swami Vivekananda

The Frog Story

Let me start with a frog-story that you may be familiar with. This was doing rounds as an email forward during the pre-whatsapp era. I got it as a forward from my friend Swamy, a banknote designer. Since the origin is not known I am not able to credit the source. I must admit that this kind of stuff comes in handy, when I run out of ideas.

A group of frogs were hopping contentedly through the woods, going about their froggy business, when two of them fell into a deep pit. All other frogs gathered around the pit to see what could be done to help their companions. When they saw how deep the pit was, the rest of the dismayed group agreed that it was hopeless and told the twosome that they should prepare themselves for their fate, because they were as good as dead. Unwilling to accept this terrible fate, the two frogs began to jump with all their might. Some of the frogs shouted in to the pit that it was hopeless and the two frogs wouldn't have been in that situation, if they had been more careful, more obedient to the froggy rules, and more responsible. The other frogs continued sorrowfully shouting that they should save their energy and give up, since they were already as good as dead. The two frogs continued jumping as hard as they could and after several hours of desperate effort, were quite weary. Finally, one of the frogs took heed to the call of his fellows. Spent and disheartened, he quietly resolved himself to his fate, lay down at the bottom of the pit and died as others looked on in helpless grief.

The other frog continued to jump with every ounce of energy he had to the point of exhaustion. His companions began anew, yelling at him to accept his fate, stop the pain and die. The weary frog jumped harder and harder and –wonder of wonders- finally leapt so high that he sprang from the pit. Amazed, the other frogs celebrated his miraculous freedom and then gathering around him asked, 'why did you continue jumping when you were told that it was impossible?' The frog was astonished when it understood what they asked and then, explained to them that he was deaf and when he saw their gestures and shouting, he thought they were cheering him on. What he had perceived as encouragement inspired him to succeed and try against all odds.

Advice- wise or vice?

Like any story, this also goes on to give the moral of the story: "there is death and life in the power of the tongue; your encouraging words can lift someone up and help him or her make it through the day and your destructive words can cause deep wounds; they may be weapons that destroy someone's desire to continue trying. And hence friends, speak words of kindness, praise or encouragement… blah.., blah…" No, I am not trying to mean that caring, kind words do not matter; rather they do matter a lot. And whether we practice or not, we all know that. (My only advice to the advisers is to leave your listeners with the story and let them derive their own advice, and then your story could be more impacting.)

Can we turn deaf to criticism?

Coming back to the frog story, there are more lessons to learn from the dead frog which could not turn deaf to the dissuasions of its on-shore colleagues. Coming to our world, let us look into our own behaviour. Can we make a choice and remain unaffected?

We saw in the last chapter we have the power to make our choice and develop the ability to respond to any negative stimulus when we create a bigger purpose for our life. Though it sounds inspiring, we find it really hard to apply it in life. We are often helpless in warding off from negative feelings, when we are faced with criticism, reprimands or failures. We feel bad when someone hurts us; we feel dejected when our request is turned down by a friend; we feel threatened when a peer is recognised for performance; we feel worried when our boss takes us to task; these habits are deep-rooted in us and we can't help these reactive habits; can we?

The habits are more like Mexican monkey trap, which is nothing but closed box with a small opening, just big enough for the monkey to slide its hand in. But once the monkey grabs a handful of nuts inside, it cannot take it hand out, for the hole is not big enough for its fist. The monkeys, being monkeys, get caught in the traps, because they do not let go off the nuts. But, we can always look in to our habitual patterns of feelings and actions and check if they are helpful for us. If they are not, we can always make a conscious choice to a new helpful feeling or behaviour, which over time will become a part of ourselves.

I can hear you: 'That's again just another metaphor, but is there practical help?' Yes, NLP can help you with the techniques to change your inner language, which can change the way you think, feel and talk to yourself.

Programming the Inner Talk

When I was in my thirties, I shifted my field of work from 'operations management' to 'human resource development (hrd). Not an easy task though, to start from scratch when you are already in an advanced stage of your career. But as I started in, the work of working with people fascinated me and I didn't mind over-stretching myself to learn anything that is new to make my training sessions interesting for the participants. That was when I came across an ad saying 'get certified in NLP and lead a powerful life'. When I got through what NLP stood for, excepting the 'linguistic' part, the other two terms 'neuro' and 'programming' were anathema to me. Not sure as to whether it was something to do with medical science or computers, I registered myself for the weekend certification course in NLP, since I felt that being 'certified' could give some clout, apart from adding a few new techniques to my training kitty.

A stocky person with a cheerful countenance, Sharma had something that attracted people. During the first session, there was more Sharma than NLP; but as he continued the stories shifted from his to ours- that of participants and each of us had some interesting or sorry tale to share. That was when I realised that NLP was not something out there, but it was about what we did with our lives and I can't be expecting someone to lecture on NLP like Physics or Philosophy. The results you are producing now whether they are positive or negative, depends largely on how you talk to yourself. If you want to change the outcomes, you need to change the way you talk to yourself. That was my understanding of NLP.

During the session, Sharma mentioned a number of books that could help in bettering ourselves and the one he laid a lot of emphasis on was a book titled 'Unlimited Power' by Anthony Robbins. Sharma said that we could get much more from this one book than from any training program.

Neuro-Linguistic Programming

First thing I did immediately after the workshop was to grab a copy of the book 'Unlimited Power'. Tony Robbins is a big fan of NLP and his book is a full-fledged workshop on NLP.

To get the essence of what NLP is all about, listen to Tony Robbins: "NLP is the study of how language, both verbal and nonverbal, affects our nervous system. Our ability to do anything in life is based upon our ability to direct our own nervous system...NLP provides a systematic framework for directing our own brain. In short, it is the science of how to run your brain in an optimal way to produce the results you desire".

I must credit my trainer not only for introducing me to 'Unlimited Power', but also the way he built in me the conviction on the seven presuppositions of NLP, which are of course, its fundamental principles. Only when you believe or at least accept the presuppositions of NLP, only then you can expect the results from using its tools and techniques. Let's see what these principles are:

1. The meaning of communication is the response you get

2. You have all the resources you need

3. Success is the ability to achieve intended results

4. There is no such thing as failure; there are only feedbacks

5. The map is not the territory

6. There is a positive intention behind every behavior

7. There are always more choices

One of the ways for getting effective outcomes is to use the 'as if' technique. Now, act 'as if' the above presuppositions are true; and you'll be surprised to find that changes your thinking, your attitude to yourself and others.

The Tony Robbins' Way

We have within us the power to make our lives better. We have the power to shape our perceptions, and to control our thoughts and behaviour. "Communication is power...Your level of communication mastery in the external world will determine your level of success with others – personally, emotionally, socially, and financially. More important, the level of success you experience internally – the happiness, joy, ecstasy, love... is the direct result of how you communicate to yourself. How you feel is not the result of what is happening in your life- it is your *interpretation* of what is happening."

USF & 7 Character Traits

Having studied a number of successful people, Tony Robbins asserts that people attain excellence by following a consistent path, which he terms as Ultimate Success Formula (USF). He succinctly captures them in four distinct steps:

Step 1: Know your outcome; define what you want precisely;

Step 2: Take action that has the greatest probability of producing the results you want;

Step 3: Take note as to whether your actions are getting you closer to what you want or further away;

Step 4 : Be flexible to change your actions until they produce the desired results.

Robbins identifies seven character traits that are commonly seen in all successful people These seven traits, he says, are the triggering mechanisms that give them the fire to do whatever it takes to succeed. *First* is Passion; passion gives the fuel that powers success and help you tap your true potential. You must love what you do; *Second* is Belief, as the famous saying of Ford goes, 'Whether you think you can, or think you can't - you're right'; *Third* is Strategy- a way of organising your resources and finding the right avenues; *Fourth* is Clarity of Values - knowing what is important to you; having a clear sense of who you are and why you do what you do; *Fifth* is Energy- "Great success is inseparable from the physical, intellectual, and spiritual energy that allows us to make the most of what we have"; *Sixth* is Bonding Power - ability to bond with people from a variety of backgrounds and beliefs; and *Seventh* is Mastery of Communication - That is essence of what the book is about: learning how to communicate with ourselves in a way that will produce results.

If you are really keen to pump power into your life and derive your desired results from your actions, Tony Robbins is the person to look to and Unlimited Power is the book to go to.

๑๑๑

Now, go beyond and read

Unlimited Power – *The New Science of Personal Achievement*

By Anthony Robbins

Thought Note

What is the inner talk going on at the moment? Do you find it helpful or is it hindering in your progress?

If you find it a hindering one, what helpful thought can you replace it with?

9
Be Your Word

Happiness is when 'what you think',
'what you say' and 'what you do' are in harmony.

- Mahatma Gandhi

'Can you submit the monthly MIS report by eod (end of the day)?' I asked Mani. He nodded with a synchronous 'yessir'. I took his words for granted and didn't check with him on the progress throughout the day. Not finding the report on my table by the eod as I was about to wind up, I thought I'd check with Mani. His colleague, who shared his intercom, answered my call saying that Mani had already left for the day. I was totally upset with his sloth. Things could have been different, had I been in my previous company. But being new to this company, I thought I should not mess it up and miss the lesson, if any, from the incident.

The next day morning, the first thing I did was to summon Mani to my cabin. As he entered my office, I found myself uttering. 'I didn't expect this from you Mani!' Despite all my conscious effort to control my emotions, the puzzled what-is-wrong look on his face annoyed me even more and I could not help the decibel level of my voice. I had to literally remind him of the report he promised to deliver by the previous evening. He instantly vomited a 'sorry sir' which came like the way he uttered the 'yessir' the previous day and went on to give me the cock and bull explanations. The more I persisted on making him realise his mistake, the more reasons and justifications he came up with.

At the end of it all, I was left bewildered by the kind of incongruence between what one says and what one does and my listening to the person altered forever. I have translated what I heard in terms of how I would listen to the person henceforth. 'Sorry sir': *I have got my reasons and will not mind repeating it in future;* 'I didn't know it was important': *I don't take whatever you assign to me as important;* When asked, 'then why did you say yes when I asked you for the report by eod?' the reply was 'How can I tell 'no' to you sir?': *'I say yes so as not to displease you;* 'you didn't later ask for the progress later during the day: *if it is important you should follow-up and not rely on my word;* 'the super boss won't ask for these reports': *I don't take your insturctions seriously.*

I remember the story of the shepherd boy who shouts 'wolf! wolf!' to trick the villagers into thinking that a wolf is attacking his flock. He repeats this so many times that the villagers stop believing any of his crap and when his sheep are actually confronted by a wolf, the villagers do not heed to his cries for help and his flock gets devoured by the wolf.

There is more to it than the simple moral that once a liar- always a liar or even a truth of a habitual liar will be treated as a lie. But a deeper insight I get now is that the world listens to me in a way that I occur to them. The world we live in is made up of different communities around us each of which has a listening of its own. And how I occur to each community will be a function of the community's past experience with me. I remember a beautiful saying 'what you are shouts so loudly into my ears that I cannot hear what you say'. The world around you treats your words from their past experience of you. What you were in the past gives the meaning to your words and not what you really say. If you have not honoured your words in the past, if you have not kept your promises, you cannot expect others to believe you will do so in future.

Is there recourse, if you genuinely want to alter the way the world sees you? Yes, you can, according to **"*The Three Laws of Performance*:** *Rewriting the Future of Your Organization and Your Life"-* a thought-provoking book by Steve Zaffron and Dave Logan. It is not about fixing your problems, but finding in yourself the power to re-write your future. Along the way, you'll likely see and transform much of what is holding you back, both professionally and personally. Zaffron and

Logan's approach to leadership is to turn conversations upside down and dig beyond the words that are said to get to what's really going on.

According to the authors, there are three laws of performance and they are:

1. How people perform correlates to how situations occur to them;

2. How a situation occurs arises in language; and

3. Future-based language transforms how situations occur to people.

How people perform correlates to how situations occur to them. Another way to say it is "There's what happens and what you make it mean." It's never what happens that upsets us – it's how we perceive what happens and how we judge what happens. It's the conversations we have with ourselves about what that means. For example, let's say that you're sitting in a room and someone gets up, leaves the room and slams the door. You might think that they were angry. What happened? They left the room. The door slammed. What you made it mean? They were angry. But see, you could be wrong. And that's where communication and perception breakdowns create a mess that no amount of skilled leadership could solve, unless you know how to manage that.

How a situation occurs, arises in language. The best way to understand this concept is with the example from the book of Helen Keller. Helen describes how she thought with her body, how she cried without understanding the emotions behind the tears. Then once she learned to communicate, a whole new world was open to her. The world literally occurred differently for her, because she could now name and communicate emotions around it.

Future-based language transforms how situations occur to people. This principle creates the distinction between describing what's there and what that means and creating and generative language. This is language that generates something new – a new future – a different experience. The theory was that when you create a new future, things that might be a problem NOW, may not be a problem in a future scenario, so you shouldn't spend time solving that.

The only way to change behaviour is to change a perception in the mind and the heart. It is no different in the field of corporate change. Most of the time top company management wants a change and forces employees to embrace the change. If the employees don't believe in the change, they will resist.

The second law is about the language we use: How the world occurs to us is a direct function of the language we use and how we view the world around us. If someone is introduced to you as a friendly person, you listen to him with great attention; if someone is introduced to you as an offensive person, you try to protect yourself from him. Thus, how we think and act is based on linguistic description -- we don't know that person is friendly or offensive. So if we can change our words, we can change our behaviour.

The third rule is about focusing on the future. If the people's thinking is locked into the past, they cannot move into the future. We can think and analyze the past, but more important we have to think about how we will create the future. The things to build our future are very different from the past because conditions and people change.

The Three Laws of Performance is a not just another must-read for every leader but a book for having organizational conversations around. When the Three Laws in this book are applied, performance transforms to a level far beyond what most people think is possible and it can happen so momentarily, as individuals and organizations rewrite their future.

৵৵৵

Now, go beyond and read

The Three Laws of Performance: Rewriting *the Future of Your Organization and Your Life*

By Steve Zaffron and Dave Logan

Thought Note

Are you aware of the times when what you did was not in sync with what you said? Do you feel the need to do something about it in future?

10
Creating a Questioning Culture

*"The most serious mistakes are not being made
as a result of wrong answers.
The true dangerous thing is asking the wrong question."*

- Peter F. Drucker

'Bhoruka Steel does it again: It has once again broken its own record and tapped the Heat in 55 minutes flat.' I still remember this ad released by a Bhoruka's supplier during the eighties. I remember this, not just because I was working for Bhorukas then, but because of the precious lessons I learnt during my initial years of my career there. The most significant one came from the production head N R Pai. Every record, the *melters* made, be it tapping the *heats* in record time (*heat* is the time taken from loading the furnace with raw materials to the time of tapping the liquid metal into the ladle) or reducing the consumption of power or materials, it can be attributed to the leadership of Pai. His style was simple- he had a way of asking questions in a very non-threatening style– to bring out the seemingly-irrelevant data, to trigger thinking and to induce learning.

Why- How Leadership

Bold red-inked 'why's marked by Pai in the previous day's log book would form the basis for most discussions during his meetings. His daily meetings with the shift manager (who took pride in calling themselves *melters*) would happen during the overlap time of first and seconds shift. Though night shift in-charges were exempted for meeting, most often they would find their way to it, not minding their weariness. Pai would swing his whys and hows between metallurgists and melters and thus melding theory and practice. Whys helped in identifying the causes for deviations and bring them into control so that the set standards were always met. When melters performed better than the standards or broke the old records, Pai never forgot to pat on their backs. But he did not stop there -he translated the new record into a new learning by asking a series of hows. The learning helped others to replicate the new record and the new record became a new standard.

Leading With Questions

My early lessons on 'leadership by questioning' got reinforced, when I happened to read the book *'Leading with Questions'* authored by Michael Marquardt, an internationally noted educator and consultant. Here are a few things I got from the book *LWQ*:

Leadership is not about knowing all the answers. It's about knowing what great questions to ask, and carefully listening to those answers. Leadership is about asking great questions – questions that inspire, motivate, and empower the organization. Astute leaders use questions to encourage full participation in teamwork, to spur innovation and outside the box thinking, to empower others, to build relationships with customers, to solve problems, and more. Questions wake people up. They prompt new ideas. They show people new places, new ways of doing things. They help us admit that we don't know all the answers. They help us become more confident communicators.

LWQ provides a comprehensive foundation on ways to employ questions effectively when leading others. The book offers a variety of principles and strategies for asking questions as well as numerous stories of how leaders have used questions to attain organizational success and personal fulfillment.

From an early age, we are discouraged from asking questions, be it at home or, school, as they are considered rude, inconsiderate, or intrusive. As we ask fewer questions, we become ever less comfortable and competent in asking questions. When we become leaders, we feel that it is important for us to have the answers rather than questions. The failure to ask questions can lead to a distorted sense of reality.

Questioning Culture

Leaders need to create a questioning climate where employees feel safe and able to trust the system and the people involved. Without this level of safety and comfort, people are generally unwilling to be vulnerable, and to be comfortable answering questions that might seem threatening. Leaders, through questions, can build a culture in which questions are welcomed, assumptions are challenged, and new ways to solve problems are explored. Questions establish an inquiring culture in organizations, and such an inquiry and culture builds a learning organization.

Questions also build a culture of accountability. When we ask questions of others and invite them to search for answers with us, we're not just sharing information, we are sharing responsibility. When responsibility is shared, ideas are shared, problems become shared-problems and not yours or mine anymore. Asking questions results in empowerment and shared ownership of results.

Six hallmarks of questioning culture

When an organization has a questioning culture, the people in it

- Are willing to admit, "I don't know."

- Go beyond allowing questions; they encourage questions.

- Are helped to develop the skills needed to ask questions in a positive way.

- Focus on asking empowering questions and avoid disempowering questions.

- Emphasize the process of asking questions and searching for answers rather than finding the "right" answers.

- Accept and reward risk taking.

Questions serve as the foundation for increasing individual, team, and organizational learning. Learning depends upon curiosity and asking questions. Questions, especially challenging ones, cause us to think and to learn. When we open our eyes and minds to the perspective of others, we open ourselves to learning.

Questions encourage and enable individuals and groups to understand, to clarify, and to open up new avenues of exploration for solving problems. They provide new insights and ideas for strategic actions and potential paths for solutions. Questions and responses to those questions provide necessary and valuable information to solve problems faster and make better decisions.

Empowering Questions

Context is the key to asking questions: "what do I want my question to accomplish?" One of the reasons that questions cause trouble is that we often ask questions that disempower others i.e. those questions that focus on the reasons why the person did not or cannot succeed, for example: Why are you behind schedule? *Empowering questions*, on the other hand, get people to think and allow them to discover their own answers, thus developing self responsibility and transference of ownership for the results. Empowering questions build positive attitudes and self esteem. Empowering questions help develop alignment within teams and draw out the optimum performance from individual members and the team as a whole. They create a high energy, high-trust environment and enable people to identify, clarify, and express their wants or needs. Such questions encourage people to take risks, nurture deep relationships, and dissolve resistance to change.

- How do you feel about the project thus far?
- How would you describe the way you want this project to turn out?
- Which of these objectives do you think will be easiest to accomplish? Which will be the most difficult?

Effective questions: Effective questions are those that accomplish their purpose as well as build a positive relationship between the questioner and the questionee. There are many types of open ended questions:

Why questions. Why questions are perhaps the most important types of open ended questions for leaders to ask as these questions force everyone to go into deeper layers of cause and effect, and of purposes and assumptions. When asking *why* questions, the leader should watch their tone of voice. The *why* question should indicate curiosity and the search for knowledge, and not anger or frustration.

Explorative questions open up new avenues and insights and lead to new explorations: have you explored or thought of?

Affective questions invite members to share feelings about an issue: How do you feel about leaving this job?

Reflective questions encourage more exploration and elaboration: You said there are difficulties with your manager; what do you think causes these difficulties?

Probing questions invite the person or group to go more deeply into a particular issue. Words such as describe, explain, clarify, elaborate, or expand get into more depth or breadth on a topic

Fresh questions challenge basic assumptions: has this ever been tried?

Questions that create connections establish a systems perspective: What are the consequences of these actions?

Analytical questions examine causes and not just symptoms: Why has this happened?

Clarifying questions help free us from ambiguity, but such questions are sometimes difficult to ask: What specifically did you mean by that?

Building a Questioning Culture

The goal for the inquiring leader is to change the corporate culture from one of *telling* to one of *asking*, to help everyone see and understand that questions need to become their primary communications tool. How can a leader develop a questioning culture? Here are some strategies that can build a powerful learning and questioning culture:

- ◆ Start at the top. The questioning culture must begin with the most senior leaders, who model the frequent use of good questions.

- ◆ Create an environment that enables the people to challenge the status quo, take risks, and ask more questions.

- ◆ Connect the values and processes of the organization to the use of questions.

- ◆ Optimize the opportunities to ask questions by building questioning into every business activity, including formal and informal meetings, sales calls, and conferences with clients, or presentations.

- ◆ Report and appreciate questioners; promote risk taking and tolerate mistakes.

- ◆ Provide training for people to be better at it and more comfortable in asking questions.

Successful leaders go beyond asking questions; they work to create an environment in which everyone can ask and be asked questions. This means, first of all, that they focus on fostering a climate where employees still feel safe in asking questions and able to trust the system and the people involved.

Now, go beyond and read

Leading With Questions -*How Leaders Find the Right Solutions by Knowing What to Ask*

By Michael Marquardt

Thought Note

Do you get a sense of your questioning style? How can you 'question' differently that can make you more effective and influential?

Ask yourself, before putting your question to others: what do I expect my question to accomplish? Frame your question such a way that it stimulates thinking and it is not seen as threatening.

11
Steering the Tough Talk

Two monologues do not make a dialogue.

- Jeff Daly

It's all about skills

"Ouch! That was pretty close, he would have killed himself," said I, as a streak of panic ran through me and I was pushing my right foot hard as though pressing the brake pedal. Raj, who was driving the car, seemed to be least perturbed. Trying to justify my apparent panic, I persisted, "these damned bikers should be shot point-blank."

"Calm down Bharath, if you have to drive on these roads, you've to get used to all these." He seemed to be making an oblique reference to my driving phobia. He continued, "And you know, the biker, who just squeezed through the gap, would not even have felt the risk you are so disturbed about."

"Do you mean he is in such a hurry to be blind to the risks he goes through" I asked, in a slightly-offended tone.

"No, he is confident of his driving and does not see any risk in the way he does it. His confidence comes from his skills," I also heard the unsaid part, "and mine from mine."

Fight or Flight

How did I miss it? This is something I keep talking about in my trainings: Lack of skills lead to poor attitude and vice versa. I am also conscious that it is my lack of driving skills that is at the root of my grumbling about the road traffic or parking space.

I thought I should not miss this moment to talk about a specific behavioural skill I had wanted Raj to develop. I broached the subject cautiously.

"Yes, I agree with you Raj. We are generally averse about doing things, which we do not know or in which we lack skills."

"For instance?" he asked in a puzzled tone.

"I hate driving because I'm no good at it and it shows in my attitude. I blame a lot of things outside me to avoid driving and when I am forced to do it, I get into the primitive 'fight or flight' instinct. And now I realise the best way or rather the only way is to get on to wheels. I mean practice."

"Yes, of course, that is true with any skill we want to develop" said he on the expected lines.

"So if we look at certain things we tend to avoid, we could probably trace it to lack of some skills at its root."

He seemed to be more mindful of his driving now, obviously not wanting to give a response. But he was intently listening. "If you have a yasnor boss (yelling at subordinate for no obvious reason), the best way to tackle is to talk it out rather than sulking about it to your friends. "

"But here you see it is not only your skills that count, boss' skills too. If he is not able to take the feedback, then you had it."

"But, so is the case with driving. When you are sure of your skills, you're confident of handling the lack of other person's. If you know to steer the talk, you don't have to bother about the lack of other person's skills."

I continued, "Avoiding something may temporarily work, since we may pretend to remain unaffected. But it could erupt one day and make us get into a sort of unexpected violent behaviour. I have seen people putting in their papers at the drop of the hat. When you look a little deeper, the 'drop of the hat' would have been just a flimsy excuse for the real reasons that have accumulated over time."

If we learn the finer way of handling these tough conversations, be it in personal or in professional relationships, we may not need to operate from the 'flight of fight' extremes or 'silent or violent' modes, as Kerry Patterson and team have termed in their book *Crucial Conversations'®*.

Why do we get stuck?

Whenever you find yourself stuck with another person or situation, it is a sure sign of a crucial conversation waiting to happen. Conversations turn crucial particularly when there are opposing viewpoints, strong emotions, and the stakes are high. Be it talking to your boss about your annual hike or discussing with your wife about her obsession of buying gold, there are certainly polar-opposite views and high stakes and no doubt, the emotions run high when these issues are taken up. Because it is tough to talk these things out, we either tend to avoid them or mess them up when we try to handle.

Repeated patterns of futile behaviour

At the first sign of a conversation going bad, we tend towards fight or flight — more commonly, experienced as moving into silence or violence. Silence and violence surface through three respective behaviours for each.

Silence is any action taken to withhold information from the pool of meaning. It ranges from playing verbal games to avoiding a person entirely. It occurs via masking, avoiding, and/or withdrawing.

- **Masking** consists of understating or selectively showing our true opinions. Sarcasm, sugarcoating, and couching are some ways we mask our meaning.

- **Avoiding** involves staying completely away from sensitive subjects. We talk—but without addressing the issues that are uncomfortable or upsetting.

- **Withdrawing** happens when we pull out of communication altogether. We lose even the possibility of dialogue by steering clear of those who might raise difficult subjects. In some cases we go so far as to withdraw from a team or a project or to transfer others in order to avoid dealing with them.

Violence can be any action taken to compel others toward your point of view. It occurs via controlling, labelling, and/or attacking.

- **Controlling** is coercing others through how we share our views or drive the conversation itself. It includes cutting others off, overstating our opinions, speaking in absolutes, forcefully changing the subject, or using directive questions to control the conversation.

◆   **Labeling** is putting a label on people or ideas so we can dismiss them under a general stereotype or category.

◆   **Attacking** is the stage of violence where we've given up on convincing other people and have adopted a goal of punishing them personally. We resort to abusive tactics such as belittling, name-calling, and threatening.

Though people tend to handle routine business communication effectively, when it comes to crucial conversations, they get bogged down and go haywire; yet such conversations have incredible potential. How people conduct themselves during these times will have a tremendous effect on a relationship, or on a company. Unfortunately, as Patterson and team write in *Crucial Conversations*, "when conversations matter the most – that is, when conversations move from casual to crucial – we're generally on our worst behaviour."

Dialoguing skill

The authors of the book discovered that most people resort to one or the other end of a scale with violence at one end and silence at the other, or what we term as the primitive 'fight or flight' mode. Flight in today's world becomes silence or absence; fight becomes yelling, screaming, pushing and other forms of violence. The worst communicators when faced with a crucial conversation run from it or escape mentally. Good communicators either sugar-coat their opinions or ramrod them. The best communicators, however, resolve the problem through *dialogue*.

Confront sarcasm with straight talk and not silence

What people need to learn is how to dialogue when a crucial conversation is imminent. "Each of us enters conversations with our own opinions, feelings, theories and experiences about the topic at hand," writes Patterson and the authors of *Crucial Conversations*. "This unique combination of thoughts and feelings makes up our personal pool of meaning ... People who are skilled at dialogue do their best to make it safe for everyone to add their meaning to the *shared* pool – even ideas that at first glance appear controversial, wrong, or are at odds with their own beliefs. Now, obviously, they don't agree with every idea; they simply do their best to ensure that all ideas find their way into the open."

And remember, 'dialoguing' cannot be mastered in a day and has to be learnt by doing like you learnt to manoeuvre your car through traffic-laden roads. The book *Crucial Conversations* can at best, serve as a manual for steering your talk.

Next time when you are stuck in a situation, just take a moment to check if there is a crucial conversation waiting to happen.

෧෧෧

Now, Go Beyond and Read

Crucial Conversations
Tools for Talking When Stakes Are High
by Kerry Patterson, Joseph Grenny, Ron McMillan, Al Switzler

Thought Note

Have you been avoiding issues needing tough talk with your peers, boss or subordinates or, with your family relatives by getting into different ways of 'silence'?

Can you think of ways to tackle them?

12
Break Rules- Build Values

"Because we cannot measure the things that have the most meaning, we give the most meaning to the things we can measure"

- Fred Hargadon

'Has he earned his today's salary?' a thought crossed my mind as I saw an employee placing his index finger on the biometric reader to record his 'out' time. This gadget was his first boss as, but for the input it provides to the payroll section, he would not get his pay bill at the end of the month. We are now so tech-enabled that we have moved from age-old punch card of the eighties, when work used to be wittily defined as 'two punches and one lunch' to biometric readers of today to enable managements babysit people and ensure they clock in on-time day in and day out. But it doesn't seem to have changed the definition much, excepting that 'punch' has been replaced by 'finger-print'. I have sometimes fantasized having gadgets for measuring 'the value one created at work during the day' to determine the pay rather than time-worn concept of 'butt-on-chair' time, as Semler puts it in his book. Let's come to it a little later after I share some of my other fantasies about work.

Fantasy Inc.

During your school days, you might have been asked to write essays on topics like, 'if you were the Prime Minister of your country' and we used to go into fantasy trips and let our thoughts run wild and crazy. The exercise was perhaps, intended to kindle the creativity in a funny way in children, but the teacher made the exercise so serious as though our lives depended on what we wrote and took away all the fun. I remember having written in one such essay in which I became the President of India and issued an order to put in jail all the teachers who cane the pupils; needless to say, how I got caned up for writing such an atrocious thought. Then on, though I had not stopped fantasizing, I had always ensured to keep my fantasies to myself. Even when I got into my job, I used to go on my fantasy trips and in one such, I became the CEO of my Company- Fantasy Inc., and wrote my rules and policies; and fortunately, to this day, no boss of mine has laid his hands on this:

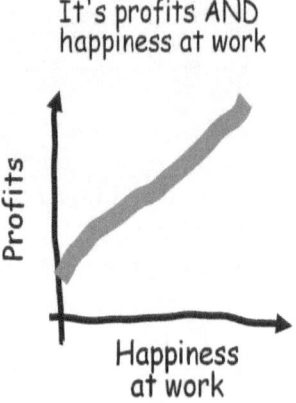

- Employees will set their own working hours
- Employees choose their own salaries
- All meetings are open to everyone
- Employees can hire their own bosses
- HR is abolished, since leaders handled all people matters
- Employees will rate their bosses and all ratings will be published
- Employees choose which leader they want to work under

- Employees choose which area of work they want to work in
- Employees can take optional holidays.
- Above all, employees will create their own rules and break them the moment they feel the rules are no more serving the intended goals or values.

Happiness as Core Value

Will you believe me, if I say all these and much more revolutionary ideas have been in practice for over three decades in one group of companies that is head quartered in Brazil. Yes, this is how business is run in one of the highly profitable companies- growing at nearly 40 percent a year- which employs over 3000 people working in three countries in manufacturing, professional services and high-tech software. You have no option but to take it, if you read the book '*The Seven Day Weekend*' written by Ricardo Semler, who has been breaking traditional business rules as the CEO Semco for over three decades. Semco, is so different, so innovative and so successful that the business world has been forced to sit up and pay attention. In his book, Semler describes how his company has changed the way of work - from boredom, monotony and repetition into joy, inspiration and freedom. Core theme of Semler's approach is that work can be made more fun, and finding a balance between work and private passions can be significantly gratifying. Having experimented with this idea, Semler advocates this philosophy, not as a lofty concept, but a better and more profitable way to do business and explains how his company has grown from $35 million in revenue to $212 million in just six years. He outlines the principles that have led the company to outstanding success while breaking every tenet in the traditional rule book.

Semco's Tenets

Semco is certainly one of the world's most unusual workplaces and the basic tenets run like these:

- Lack of formal structure- willingness to let workers follow their interests and instincts when choosing their jobs or projects;
- Insistence that workers seek personal challenges and satisfaction before even trying to meet the company's goals;

- Commitment to encourage employees ramble through their day or week so that they will meander into new ideas and new business opportunities;

- Philososphy of embracing democracy and open communication, and inciting questions and dissent in the workplace.

If all these sound too-utopian and weird, have a look at some of the initiatives that are actually being practiced at Semco. They might, for sure, sound weird to our, what Semler calls 'calcified' thinking, the state of mind where ideas have become so hardened that they are no longer of any use. Here are some of Semco's innovative initiatives, which would make many CEOs awestruck:

Up'n Down pay – is a program where employees flexibly manage their pay. The idea is that moments in people's lives are very different, one from the other – and that making it possible for them to adapt their pay and work hours accordingly. Employees would look to balance the company's present needs with their own, and adjust the pay package accordingly.

Retire-A-Little – is a program where employees are free to retire at any age and work at the later stages of their lives. People can retire for a two months period now and work two months after their retirement.

Work'n Stop plan - is a program where employees can take off longer periods (upto 3 years) for reasons of realizing dream, study, and travel or re-evaluate life. Along with 11 different ways Semco has for remunerating people, these programs make it easy to stay at Semco for decades, without forcing difficult choices on people when they yearn to take a break, go back to school, or have a family.

Go/No Go Meetings – is a philosophy where, if anyone calls for a meeting, you have the right to vote whether to go or not to go. If most of the employees turn down the meeting request, it means the meeting is not much of important or the new idea is not appealing.

Do nothing - is a philosophy to govern at Semco. In crisis or when something breaks down, the senior management will be at their best to do...nothing. This is because, by doing nothing, employees will be at their best to manage their crisis and there evolves the leadership.

Why, why, why? – is the way every point is addressed in the meeting. By questioning repeatedly, they will come up with a new idea with a convincing strategy to crack the same.

These are only a small sample of the revolutionary ways in which Semco operates. Semco keeps going on - constantly questioning the way they do things- experimenting with newer ways of turning work into an experience of fun, inspiration and freedom – and in the process, making more and more money too.

Semler believes central purpose of business is "a satisfying, worthwhile life for those involved and a reasonable reward for their investment and hard work". Semler explains that allowing the employees to manage themselves is a business model that has not only worked for Semco, but could be put into use at any organization that wants to move beyond traditional thinking into a more democratic realm.

By now, you must either be too tempted to go and grab the book or feel too far-removed to kick it aside as too sour a bunch of grapes to reach.

ক঩ক঩ক঩

Now, go beyond and read

The Seven-Day Weekend

by Ricardo Semler

Thought Note

How do you fantasise a great place to work? Are there things you can do to create a fantastic workplace?

13
The Becoming

"Where the mind is lead forward by Thee into ever
widening thought and action,
Into that heaven of freedom, my father,
let my country awake."

- Rabindranath Tagore

'You have hardly spent a year in your present job which you got just after completing your engineering degree. Why do you want to change your job so soon?' I asked candidate who had walked in for an interview. 'I would like to work for a professional company' he replied. When I asked him further as to why he thought his present employer was not one, he was quick to say 'I am the only professional in my department, no other person, not even my boss has a professional degree'. To him, professionalism did not mean anything beyond having a professional degree or qualification.

Though my immediate reaction was one of annoyance, rebuke and pity for the kind of professionals our colleges are turning out, I quickly realised that my own definition of professional was far from perfection and needed refinement. If the candidate had the guts to turn back and ask me, 'then, can you tell me what it means 'to be a professional?', I am not sure what I would have blurted. I could have at the most, said "what being a professional is not: it is not mere having a professional degree;

it's not about just gaining expertise in one's subject; it's just not about the ability to flaunt the jargons in one's talk'. Probably, I could have given some examples of the people, who I thought of as real professionals. But how exactly I would define a professional - I was not sure. I felt a bit embarrassed by this thought –not for my ignorance- but for the way I felt about the candidate. Education, as someone said, is a progressive realisation of ignorance and this kind of disturbances help me focus my learning. This jolt is often, the place we move from 'I don't know that I don't know' to 'I know that I don't know'- Remember, we talked about this in an earlier chapter.

When I was scanning the bookshelves at Higginbothams, I immediately pulled out the book with red jacket that adorned the silvery letters THE PROFESSIONAL on its spine. While the title caught my attention, the author Subroto Bagchi enticed me to start reading it instantly. I have always been captivated by his columns that used to appear in Times of India. His writings have the simplicity of words, clarity of thoughts and more importantly, a profound authenticity of expression which make them touching and inspiring.

Unlettered Professional

As is my wont, I started reading the book page by page rather than skimming through. Bagchi opens the book with the chapter 'Burial of the dead'. He very succinctly brings out the idea of who a true professional is in the first four pages of the book itself. He narrates the story of a real life character Mahadeva, whose life is dealing with unclaimed dead bodies. This is not someone who is conventionally associated with the term 'Professional'. He grew up uncared for in the vicinity of a hospital right from his early age, since his old and delirious mother was under the care of the hospital. One day it so happened that the police asked him to bury an unclaimed dead body for a meager fee and from then on, he became the go-to guy for burying the city's unclaimed corpses.

Every time the police picked up a dead body that had no claimants, Mahadeva was summoned. Whenever he got a call to reach the morgue, day or night, hail or high water, he arrived. Most of the time, it was gruesome experience dealing with a dead body; there was no telling what had been the cause of death or state of decomposition. He did not choose his clients; he accepted them in whatever size, shape or state they came; he treated them with respect and care, with due dignity. He was not an employee of the hospital, nor did the cops supervise what he did with the corpses. He did not have a boss who wrote his appraisal or gave feedback. He did his work with such dedication, focus, care and concern that he was so much in demand. Mahadeva has buried more than 42000 corpses in his lifetime and his dedication has earned him phenomenal public recognition.

Differentiating qualities

From the story of Mahadeva, Bagchi brings out the two qualities that differentiate a professional from someone who is simply professionally qualified: one is the ability to work unsupervised and, two, the ability to certify the completion of one's work. If you have to get the complete sense of what I have tried to comprehend, there is no better way than reading the book. The story was so moving that I could not help tears welling in my eyes as I was reading it. I am sure that the story of Mahadeva, a professional in the truest sense of the word, will always remain in the heart of every professional, who reads the book.

Integrity- Hallmark of a true Professional

I find the master storyteller in Bagchi, as he spins the real life incidences of his rich and multi-faceted experience into enthralling stories and there cannot be subtler ways for driving the lessons for making of a professional.

When he shares his personal life experiences that imbued in him the quality of integrity, I, as a trainer, wonder as to how I would be able to help my learners imbibe this quality- what does integrity mean in actionable terms. He comes out with help: In the professional context, it means:

- We follow rules
- Where rules do not exist, we use fair judgment
- When in doubt, we do not go ahead and do what suits us; we seek counsel
- Finally, faced with a dilemma, we ask ourselves: can my act stand public scrutiny without causing embarrassment to me and my family?

He says that if these four tenets are applied, our professional conduct will always meet the highest standards of integrity.

Professional Qualities

In writing this book, Bagchi has done his own research to find out from eminent men and women from different walks of life whom he came across in the course of his work as to what qualities they admired in a professional and what they considered unprofessional. From what he has collated from their feedback, here are the top ten attributes of a professional:

1. Integrity
2. Commitment and Ownership
3. Action orientation and goal seeking
4. Continuous learning
5. Professional Knowledge
6. Communication
7. Planning, Organizing and Punctuality
8. Quality of work
9. A positive attitude, approachability, responsiveness
10. Being an inspiring reference to others; thought leadership

While referring to the last attribute of 'being an inspiring reference to others', he says that tomorrow's professional must have a beacon-like presence in a world that will ask for memorability and being ordinary will no longer be considered professional.

The Unprofessional

He has also presented the ten markers of unprofessional conduct in the subsequent chapter. The best place to start with is to eradicate all the unprofessional behaviors that can be very unbecoming of a professional. Here is his list of unprofessional ten:

1. Missing deadline
2. Failing to be forthright
3. Withholding information to the recipient of service about the conflicting interests
4. Not respecting privacy of information that must be held in confidence

5. Not respecting 'Need to Know'

6. Plagiarizing

7. Passing the Blame

8. Overstating qualifications and experience

9. Frequently changing jobs

10. Not Taking care of your Appearance

Building a Professional Culture

Bagchi has presented The Professional in a sequentially-arranged manner under seven broad parts, namely, Integrity, Self-Awareness, Professional Qualities, Managing Volume, Managing complexity, New world imperatives and The professional's professional.

The development of a professional is a life-long learning curve and there is no beginning or end in this pursuit. Reading the book alone cannot make one a professional. But it is about being one. And as Bagchi concludes, being a professional is a matter of personal choice and the values one opts to live by.

If you want to build a professional culture in your organisation, you have to engage in a collective conversation on the various aspects of being professional so as to commonalise the understanding. That's how the organization can learn to be professional.

ఈఈఈ

Now, go beyond and read

The Professional –*Defining the New Standard of Excellence at Work*
by Subroto Bagchi

Thought Note

How do you see yourself as a professional? How can you build your professional image?

14
Standout with S.M.A.R.T. Tools

*We become what we behold. We shape our tools
and then our tools shape us.*

- Marshall McLuhan

Power of Acronyms

Ram, the brand manager in the company I work, has this crazy habit of expanding the initials of every person he meets in to some funny phrase. Though the expansions may sound a bit weird, they were always positive and made the other person feel good. For instance, when I got introduced to him, he called me by my initials GB and said, 'GB, Go Beyond'. That really caught on quickly with all my colleagues and soon many started calling me GB.

Ram's style of turning initials into acronyms established two things for me: one, is he had become quickly familiar with most people in a short time, and two, he also had established himself as someone different which was also essential for the nature of work he was involved in: brand management.

One thing I learned in the whole process was the power of acronym in helping remember things. And one thing I must confess to Ram before he reads this is the expansion we secretly use for his name: Random AcronyManiac.

Acronym as Hooks

The teachers who make learning fun or easy are remembered long. I remember a particular chemistry teacher, who gave me this crazy but indelible phrase: *'Leo says Ger'*. This helped me in clearing the confusion between oxidation and reduction. Though these basic concepts of chemistry have nothing to do with my job for the last thirty years, I can't forget even today that *Loss of electrons is Oxidation (LeO) and Gain of electrons is Reduction (GeR)*. That is the power of acronyms. It's jovially said of a doctor who instructed his patient not to think of the monkey when he takes the medicine. The patient just can't help thinking of the monkey whenever he takes medicine, because he's conscious of what he should not be conscious of.

Acronyms work in a similar fashion. Use of acronyms is one effective way for registering things in our memory. The alphabets of the acronym serve like hooks on which the words connected to them are hung. The moment you get the acronym, the related words pop out as though they were hanging on the hooks.

SMART as memory hooks

S.M.A.R.T. is an acronym popularly associated with 'smart goals'. Smart is often used to denote the five vital criteria one should remember while setting goals, i.e. specific, measurable, achievable, realistic and time-bound and this has become so very fundamental that there are so now many variations of it on internet. Smart goals always fascinated me for both the word and the acronym stood to represent the same thing. My fascination to use smart as acronym grew when I was preparing for the workshop on presentation skills titled 'Smart Presenter'. I continued with my saga of smarting, un-smarting and re-smarting various concepts, tools and techniques which of course, were further bettered by the enthusiastic participants who came to my training. And culmination of this smart saga is a collection of 50 Smart Tools for the Professional, where I have used the alphabets in SMART as memory hooks for a wide array of mind tools that have utility in various domains of professional life.

What are Mind Tools?

We have all had some experience of using a physical tool. We use hammer to drive a nail into the wall, but all it does is to converge the force so pointedly to make the job easier. Like the physical tools serve as extension of human body that enable us do things that cannot be done otherwise, the mind tools expand our mental abilities and facilitate effective use of our mental processes. There are many mind tools which we may be using without even realising we are using one. For instance, the Things-To-Do list is a mind tool that helps us remember and prioritize our schedule for the day. Brainstorming is a mind tool that triggers generation of divergent and creative ideas on a specific theme. Fish bone diagram is a mind tool that helps mapping and classifying the causes for a particular problem. Edward De Bono has created a number of thinking tools and his "Six Thinking Hats" is a powerful mind tool for directing our thinking.

Why Hooks for Mind Tools?

We all know a good number of useful techniques (what we call as mind-tools) for every imaginable situation in our life time. But the difficulty is to ferret out the right technique at the right time from the clutter of our mental attic. For instance, imagine any of these situations: you are delivering a talk on stage, or you are engaged in a conversation and you want to say 'an emphatic No'. But the problem is you are not able to recall those useful techniques you know. I don't blame it on my memory. Given enough time, you will get them, but the problem is about recalling them quickly at the right point. So, we need some memory hooks that help us quickly recall the tools and techniques we already know. It calls for installing some kind of search engine in our mind that could google and throw up the items we want with the help of one or two key words. The alphabets of the acronym SMART serve as hooks to all the mind tools that have been developed.

Some SMART tools

Let me share a sample of few SMART tools that could be useful to you in your professional life. The smart tools are self explanatory by themselves and do not need any elaborate explanation:

1. Values Credo of a Professional

A professional needs to build his credibility and reputation by practicing what he preaches; by walking the talk. So, you need to hold a basic tenet of honouring your word. Every time, you fail to keep your spoken word, the new commitments you make will not be taken seriously and you will be seen as your past and not as your spoken word. Hence, it is very primary that you honour our spoken word, without which you will tend to lose your credibility.

Your reputation is not built in a day. It takes time and it comes with the consistent character we display in keeping up our spoken word, meeting the expectations of key stake-holders, delivering on our promises to the best of our ability and to completion. If you can live up to the SMART credo, you will surely emerge as the epitome of professionalism. The SMART values credo can be captured in these five smart words:

- **S**aid
- **M**eant
- **A**bility
- **R**epute
- **T**otality

Here is a simple definition for each of the above words that form part of Professional's SMART credo:

Said: I will do what I **Said** I will do; My Word is my commitment; I will do whatever it takes to keep and honour my Word.

Meant: I will do what I am **Meant** to do; I will fulfil what is implied and expected, though unsaid.

Ability: I will do it to the best of my **Ability;** I will give it all to walk extra mile every time.

Repute: I will do it to my **Repute;** for I understand it's about my stature and character.

Totality: I will do it to the **Totality;** completing the task undertaken gives me the professional satisfaction.

2. How to Smart-read a Book

In chapter 1, we talked about reading for results. If we want to derive benefits from the self improvement books we read, we cannot read them like novels. We have to develop some discipline in the way we read them like jotting down the points, sharing our thoughts and insights with our close-ones and, more importantly, taking action. You will find the SMART strategies can help in implementing your reading effectively.

* **S**kim
* **M**ark
* **A**bsorb
* **R**ecord
* **T**alk

Here's a brief explanation for the smart-read tool:

Skim: Reading the entire book at one go does not help. Instead skim through the book to get an idea of how it is going to help – which parts could be of real interest and relevance to you and where you would like to focus on.

Mark: Personalise the book. Use a highlighter to Mark or highlight those points you feel important and also make it a point to note the insights you get as you read on the margins of the book.

Absorb: Re-read those areas of relevance to you and think of how you will apply the idea, concept or technique to your situation.

Record: It can be of great value to maintain a personal journal to record your experience in developing a new habit or adopting a new practice. It requires a tremendous amount of discipline, but in the longer run, you can reap amazing results, for it will bring in you a new level of awareness that helps in personal growth.

Talk: Choose to talk to people in your life about the new idea you have read or what you have started practising recently. This not only helps in reinforcing and internalising what you read, but also creates a commitment in you to follow what you said.

3. Master Your Story To Ace the BEI Interview

BEI or Behavioural Event Interviews are the order of the day. In BEIs, the interviewers are no more interested in knowing your hypothetical answers and ideological solutions. They want to know what you have done in the past, for the past could be a good predictor of the future. If you have done a particular thing well in the past, then there is a fair chance of your doing so in the future too. So, the questions will focus on your past performance. For handling this type of questions, it is not enough if you have had enough sparks of performance, but you also need to narrate them interestingly well and with authenticity. For instance, if the interviewers want to know how well you handle trouble-shooting, you should be able to tell any specific instance in the past where you have done trouble-shooting well.

A simple smart structure can help in putting any such sparks of performance from your past in a coherent and interesting manner. Here is how you can structure your story:

- **S**ituation
- i**M**pediment
- **A**ction
- **R**esults
- **T**ake away

Here's a brief explanation for telling your smart story:

Situation: What was the situation, you were caught up in? When? Who were there? How did it look?

iMpediment: What was the major block or impediment you faced? What was stopping you from achieving your goal?

Action: What did you do? How did you respond to the challenge? What choices you made? What actions you took?

Results: How did it go? Did you succeed or fail in dealing with the situation?

Take away: How did you deal with the success / failure? What were you left with for the future?

4. Smart way to Understand Your Job-role

When you take up a job for the first time or transition to a new job, it is important to understand about the organisation and the practices prevalent in it, the purpose of your job and the people you will be working with, the responsibilities and deliverables of your role. No organisation gives all these to you on a platter and in most places, there may not even be any systematic documentation of all these. Hence, it is in your interest that you need to ask people and find out to develop an understanding of your role, your job, your team and your organisation. But it is certainly worth the effort, if you are planning to have a long term career.

To put it short and smart, what you should understand about your Job-role:

- **S**tructure & **S**ystems
- **M**eaning & **M**en (people)

- **A**uthority & **A**ccountability
- **R**oles & **R**esponsibilities
- **T**asks & **T**argets

Here's a brief explanation for the smart way to understand your job role:

Structure & Systems: What is the organisation structure? Whom do you report to? Who report to you? Who are your immediate customers and suppliers in the value chain?

Meaning & Men (people): Do you have a Job Description? Is there a purpose statement? What is the main purpose of the job you are holding? Who are the people you will be working with? Who are in your team? Who are your customers (internal or external), who will use your work and suppliers (internal or external) who will provide you with what you need?

Authority & Accountability: What results are you expected to deliver? What authority is vested in the position to meet your deliverables?

Roles & Responsibilities: What is your role and what duties are associated with your role? What resources are you responsible for?

Tasks & Targets: What are the key tasks in your role and what are the standards and targets for these tasks? How will your performance in these tasks be measured?

If you find the above SMART tools of value in enhancing your professional effectiveness, you can look forward to the soon-to-be launched book by the author titled *'Standout with SMART Tools'*. If you have any comments to make or a similar tool to share, get in touch with the author.

∽๑∽๑∽๑

Look forward to an upcoming book (to be released shortly) by the author:

Stand Out With SMART Tools – *50 Tools & Techniques for Professional Excellence*

By Bharath Gopalan

Thought Note

Can you tell a SMART story?

Think of a particular skill or quality in you and spin a story around it. Tell your story to someone close to you (pal) and take feedback to improve on it.

15
You Feel...Therefore You Are...

*"Holding onto anger is like drinking poison
and expecting the other person to die."*

- Gautama Buddha

Why we do what we do?

Let me start with a small episode that is supposed to be a joke: A passenger was travelling in a cab sitting in the rear seat. When he arrived near his destination point, he gently touched the driver's shoulder to indicate to him to stop. All at once, the driver screamed, turned the steering wildly to left, nearly hit a bus, turned it right, went upon the footpath and stopped close to a shop window. For a second everything was quiet in the cab, then the driver said to the passenger, "Look, don't ever do that again. You scared me so much!" The passenger apologized and said, "I never knew that a slight touch would scare you so much!" The driver replied, "Sorry, it's not really your fault. Today is my first day as a cab driver. For the last 25 years, I've been driving mortuary van that carried corpses"

Do you find it witty? Honestly, I do not. Maybe, I have a poor sense of humour. I was rather, caught up in a train of thoughts. What struck me was the driver's self-awareness. Were he not aware of what caused the panic in him, he would have gone on to find something outside him to rationalize his erratic behaviour. If he was not sure why he behaved abnormally, he would have entertained himself to put the blame outside: 'why these passengers are so insensible- don't they know this least that distracting one's attention while driving can turn out to be disastrous?' Then he would have happily(?) gone on with the abnormal behaviour.

Don't we have a situation like that? You can recall at least one situation in which you did something and then said to yourself, "Why did I do that?" These situations may arise when we are not aware of our patterns of behaviour and the underlying emotions. Becoming aware of and recognizing patterns of responses to various situations is one of the prerequisites to having some control over reactions and increasing self-directedness.

Interpersonal Competence

We spend a great deal of our time talking with people in our professional and personal life. We talk to our family members, our friends, to our peers, teammates and the customers at the workplace, and to quite a number of other people we come across in daily life. These interactions with other human beings constitute a good part of our daily experiences. You would have noticed that some of the experiences have turned quite pleasant and the relationships have flourished over time. But some others have remained stagnant or have worsened or for that matter, have even been abandoned. Have you ever looked into how and why these have happened? Such an introspective process can help in improving our relationships with others. 'Interpersonal competence' refers to the extent to which we are aware of our impact on others and of the impact of others on us. Interpersonal competence is a pre-requisite for our professional effectiveness and is a key skill for achieving our personal as well as professional goals.

Emotional Intelligence

Your interpersonal effectiveness depends, to very large extent on Emotional Intelligence Quotient, what has come to be known as EQ. The term 'Emotional Intelligence' became widely-known worldwide only after the release of Dr. Daniel Goleman's book titled *'Emotional Intelligence'* in 1995, though the concept was prevalent among social scientists and researchers much before this book. Dr Goleman is an American Psychologist, who has worked extensively on Emotional Intelligence and has authored a number of best-selling books on the subject, including *"Working With Emotional Intelligence"*, *"Social Intelligence: The New Science of Human Relationships"* and the recent one, *"Focus: The Hidden Driver of Excellence"*

Emotional intelligence is "the ability to sense, understand, and effectively apply the power and acumen of emotions as a source of human energy, information, connection and influence." To put in simple terms, it is the ability to recognize your emotions, understand what they're telling you, and realize how your emotions affect people around you. It also involves your perception of others' emotions; when you are able get a hang of how others feel, it helps you manage relationships better.

The Science of Emotional Intelligence

One good thing about Emotional Intelligence is that it is learnable, which means that you can work towards raising your EQ levels. Let's first understand the basic components of Emotional Intelligence:

1. **Self-Awareness** is your ability to recognize and understand your moods, emotions and drives; how they affect you and your work performance, your relationships with others. When you are self-aware, you can evaluate your strengths and limitations and you also experience a positive sense of self-worth. Emotional literacy is primary to developing our self awareness.

2. **Self-Management** is about your ability to control your emotions and keep yourself self-motivated; you are able to postpone self-gratification and subordinate your immediate pleasures to long-term goals and success. Self management involves Trustworthiness, Conscientiousness, Adaptability, Achievement Orientation and Initiative and this is how Goleman defines each of them:

   - Self-control is the ability to keep disruptive emotions and impulses under control.

   - Trustworthiness means a consistent display of honesty and integrity.

   - Conscientiousness is the ability to manage yourself and your responsibilities.

   - Adaptability is the skill at adjusting to changing situations and overcoming obstacles.

-   Achievement Orientation involves the drive to meet an internal standard of excellence.

-   Initiative is the readiness to seize opportunities.

3. **Social Awareness:** Empathy is an important part of Social Awareness. Empathy is the ability to identify with and understand other people's emotions- their wants, needs and viewpoints- and taking an active interest in their concerns. Highly empathetic people are able to build excellent relationships by the virtue of their ability to listen and to relate well with others.

Social Awareness also includes organizational awareness and social orientation: Organisational awareness is the ability to read the currents of organizational life and build decision networks; Service orientation is the ability to recognize and meet customers' needs.

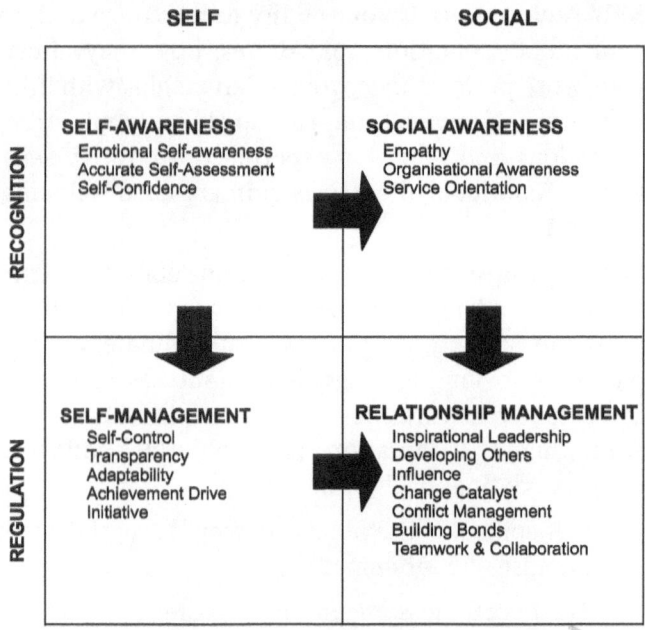

4. **Social Skills:** involves a wide range of skills comprising visionary leadership, influence, developing others, communication, change catalyst, conflict management,

building bonds, teamwork and collaboration.

- Visionary leadership is the ability to take charge and inspire with a compelling vision.

- Influence is the ability to wield a wide range of persuasive tactics.

- Developing others is the propensity to bolster the abilities of others through feedback and guidance.

- Change catalyst is the proficiency in initiating new ideas and leading people in new direction.

- Conflict management is the ability to de-escalate disagreements and orchestrate resolutions.

Here are some tips for developing emotional intelligence:

a) **Developing Emotional Self-Awareness:** Whenever you feel a feeling that you are not comfortable with, start asking yourself, 'what is this feeling telling me?' There is some message behind every emotion - it's about something that's happening now, or that has happened in the past that you have not fully resolved. You can develop your emotional awareness by thinking about your feeling to make sense of its message.

b) **Take Responsibility for Feelings:** We often try to consider certain emotions as unacceptable and we refuse to acknowledge them. Though we are in denial of our emotions, we still continue to act from those emotions. We even project it on other people. For instance, if you are in denial of your anger, you will come across a lot of angry people. So, taking responsibility for your feelings and accepting them as yours is very vital to be emotionally intelligent.

c) **Remember - You Are Not Your Feeling:** Don't judge yourself by your emotions and feeling an emotion does not make you good or bad. For that matter, no emotion is bad by itself. Whatever emotion you feel, it is only giving you some important information about the situation that you're in or about something that's happened in the past that you need to learn from and move on. A trap that we often fall into is feeling that we 'ought' to feel a certain way. We have been brought up to believe that certain emotions are wrong to express or even to feel. Remember, it's how you respond to those feelings that matters. Whatever emotion you're feeling, you still have a choice about how you act on it - and that's what counts.

d) **Put Yourself In The Other Person's Shoes:** One vital quality that can help you in building relationships or, resolving conflicts is your ability to see and understand the other person's point of view. This is particularly important when you are discussing any crucial issue with people. The best way to be conscious of other person's perspectives is to ask yourself every now and then, "What's going on for this person right now? What's important to them? What do they want from this interchange? What might they be feeling?" If you get a sense of what's going on for them, you will find them much easier to communicate with.

e) **Become Emotional-literate:** Being in touch with emotions is not an easy task amidst our hectic daily routines. But we often use the hustle-bustle of our life as an excuse to repress our feelings and escape from our conscious connection with them. But consider these: your emotions are spontaneous expression of how you relate to the people and the heppenings; you are the totality of all the relationships you have, and the most accurate mirror of them is your emotions. Hence, there is nothing more important than experiencing your feelings.

f) **Get present to your feelings:** Simply make a list of some key emotions and note one example of each as it arises in your day. Start with key words for the basic positive emotions: Love, Joy, Sympathy, Acceptance, Happiness, Friendliness, Trust and Compassion. Next, make a column for more abstract feelings associated with creativity and personal growth: Insight, Intuition, Discovery, Transcendence, Faith, Forgiveness, Peace, and Revelation. Last, note the primary negative emotions: Anger, Envy, Anxiety, Sorrow, Guilt, Greediness, Distrust and Selfishness. As you start this exercise, you will start noticing: - how often you feel things that get overlooked; - the spontaneous release of emotions that you would normally repress or try to forget; - that you are able to know your emotions and name them.

g) **Connect with your emotions:** For many, it may be difficult to specifically describe 'how a particular emotion, for instance compassion feels like'. But by consciously being on the lookout for an emotion, you will get to know it intimately. This is the first stage of mastering your emotions. The life of feelings is meant to be rich and satisfying, but if your emotions are strangers to you, you cannot enjoy them. Despite our efforts to repress them, there is a feeling attached to every single thought we have. Bringing all these feelings to light puts you back into the wholeness of the mind-body connection, and wholeness is the most satisfying state in which to live.

h) **Tackle the negative emotions:** The purpose of the exercise is to awaken the expansive, creative emotions. Negative emotions are easy to feel and they limit us – our world. Hence, it's important not to focus too much on negative emotions, which are the easiest for everyone to experience. When you are aware of where an emotion comes from, it helps in dissipation of negative feelings; gaining an insight into the origin of negative emotions helps you take the essential action to tackle them.

i) **Focus on those you want to grow:** As you practice this, you will be amazed at the range of diverse emotions you experience during the day and you will wonder how you missed them all these years. Whatever you focus upon grows; if you want to be 'grateful' or 'curious', just stay focused by looking at that word in your list for a few seconds in the morning; you will create space for them to grow. As you grow in practice, you can even move on to emotions that you may hardly feel like 'insight' or 'revelation' and you may be able to activate those emotions too in your life.

◈◈◈

Now, go beyond and read

Emotional Intelligence - *Why It Can Matter More Than IQ*

By Daniel Goleman

&

Working with Emotional Intelligence

By Daniel Goleman

Thought Note

Can you become aware of the emotion you are feeling right now?

Whenever you feel low, ask yourself: How am I feeling? What is this emotion telling me? What can I do to feel better?

16
De-role Yourself

"Many people live as if life were a dress rehearsal for some later date."

- Richard Carlson

"Bharath, please come out of the role! You are not the salesman anymore. You are Bharath attending this training course!" thundered Himanshu standing right in front of me. Momentarily, I realized that the angry salesman was still in me, holding some grudge against his boss i.e., my co-participant Jacob, who played the sales manager's role in a five minute Role Play session. When Himanshu's words struck my ears, I shook my head and laughed at myself. I rose from my seat, went and shook hands with Jacob deliberately. By this, Himanshu had just demonstrated how important it is to de-role the participants after "Role-play" session. Role-play, as you may be aware, is an experiential learning method where a set of participants are asked to enact certain pre-assigned roles in a given situation and post the Role-play, the debriefing is done to analyse the experience and bring the learning out of the exercise. By 'De-roling', the trainer brings the role-players back into their seats as learners without getting stuck with the temporary roles they had assumed in the Role-play.

Role-trapped

But I was left with a bigger learning that day. When I realized that even a few minutes of playing an artificial role can affect us emotionally and unless we consciously try and come out, it can leave lasting effect on us, without our even being aware of it. This being the case, what could be the impact of the incidents we go through day in and day out, where we get emotionally involved? I realized that this de-roling has a larger connotation beyond Roleplay and can significantly help in understanding and altering our mood swings in our real lives.

Become conscious

Some evenings, when I return home after work, I feel completely drained for no specific reason. I have remained clueless as to why I was feeling low on a particular evening and the compromise I used to make is that mood is like the climate and can get cloudy some days. But when I started making a conscious search for the root-cause of such mood swings, most often it would be a trivial incident or even a momentary gesture of some stranger which would have done the spoilsport. For instance, if I didn't heed to non-stop honking of an impatient car-driver, who wouldn't wait for the signal to turn green, I need not have to be bothered about his rude gestures. But I did and that showed up in my mood.

How to De-role

As we live our day out, we take upon us different roles at different times with different people- some roles for a short while, some endure longer and some are for lifetime. As we move from one role to another, we often, are still left with the emotional after-effects of the previous role. The residues of a yelling boss or an irate customer may remain long beyond the event and may be draining all your mental and physical energies. How do you get out of this small stuff before they turn into big stuff in our minds? When it comes to this kind of small stuff, don't go to big gurus who'd talk big stuff like yoga, meditation etc, ad nauseam but listen to the master of Small Stuff, Richard Carlson. I have always admired the simplicity of his approach and his two-pagers running to hundred give very practical ways to get over the small stuff. Here are a few from *his hundred* that can help you de-role yourself out of the small stuff.

Hundred years from now: The fact that a hundred years from now we will all be gone from this planet can add a great deal of perspective to our lives. What, if someone acted little unkindly toward you or if you had to listen to some unwanted advice? How would it matter a hundred years from now?

Choose your battles wisely: There will be times, when you will want or need to argue, confront or fight for something you believe in. Many people, however, turn their lives in to a series of battles by arguing and fighting over practically everything. It can lead to losing track of what is truly relevant. There will always be people who disagree with you and people who do things differently. Is it really important for you to prove to everyone that you are right and they are wrong? A more peaceful way is to choose consciously which battles are worth fighting for and which are better left alone.

Lighten up: These days, almost all of us seem to be too serious and bothered about almost everything –being stuck in traffic, witnessing someone look at us wrong or say the wrong thing, waiting in line and so on. The root of it is our unwillingness to accept life as being different, in any way, from our expectations. We spend our lives wanting things, people and events to be just the way we want them to be – and when they are not, we fight and suffer. A good exercise is to try to approach every single day without expectations. Don't expect people to be friendly. When they are not, you won't be bothered. If they are, you will be surprised.

Drop the ball: If someone throws the ball at you, you don't have to catch it. It is a normal tendency when someone throws you a concern, you must catch it and respond. You need to remember that you have a choice. Answering a phone when you are really busy is a form of catching the ball. By answering the phone, you are willingly taking part in an interaction you may not have time or energy at that point of time. By choosing not to answer the phone, you are taking responsibility for your own peace of mind. The same idea applies to being insulted or criticized. When someone throws the idea or comment in your direction, you can catch it and feel hurt, or you can drop it and go on your way.

Next time when you find yourself emotionally trapped, tell yourself, 'hey, come out of the role!'

ఆ◦ఆ◦ఆ

Now, go beyond and read

Don't Sweat The Small Stuff, It's All Small Stuff ...
By Richard Carlson

Thought Note

Are you able to keep your mind free of office botherations, when you are at home and engage yourself usefully? Do you enjoy quality-time with your family?

If No, what strategies you want to adopt to overcome the situation?

17

Be a Pygmalion: Grow People

*"The best brains of the nation may be found
on the last benches of the class room"*

- A.P.J. Abdul Kalam

Hiring Ritual

I hastened Rakesh to fill in the jaf quickly. Rakesh had walked in to our office twice before for the earlier rounds of interview for a team-lead position in marketing. He had to be put before the company president Keshab Nand (KN or Prez) today for the final discussions. The jafs are supposed to be filled in by the candidates in their own handwriting before they are taken for final interview. If you are wondering what this jaf is, then my purpose is served. Acronymising and jargonising the common terms are among the clever devises, we-HR pros, tend to come up with every now and then so as to give a pretence of domain specialism, lest HR becomes an easy prey for encroachment from non-HR-lot.

Prez's nod is a crucial step before the candidate is offered fitment. Though this final interview is more of a formality, KN's uncanny knack for spotting the unspotted could, at times, bring up some surprises and would put us back to ground zero of starting the whole process all over again. KN had told me the previous day that first thing he would do today was to meet the candidate. I know if I don't put Rakesh to him right in the morning, he would get into the thick of day's business and it'd not be easy to strip himself out from that later. That was why I was rushing Rakesh to complete the jaf, which, if you have not guessed by now, stands for job application form.

As Rakesh was scribbling his signature on the fourth page of the form, I discourteously pulled it out from below his pen like an exam invigilator, since KN had already walked in to his office. When I entered KN's office, he was pouring his black coffee from the flask and noticing me at the door, he asked, 'has Rakesh arrived?' Had he not, that would be enough to write him off. Not keeping time is not to be brooked at the entry stage. 'Yes Sir' I said. I could see my overstressed 'sir' sounding pungent in my ears. Though KN is liberal about being on first-name terms even with his junior colleagues, we have been hanging on to sir-culture so that the other old-timers did not get offended. As he settled down in his chair with his coffee, I placed the filled-in jaf on his table along with the ief that has already been signed off by the previous panellists with their ratings.

Graphology Bias

Giving a cursory glance at the jaf, he said, 'what Bharath, don't you know that marketing people need to be outgoing and sociable? Rakesh doesn't seem to fit the bill. He seems to be a hardcore introvert. Didn't you get it on seeing his form?' I was trying to guess whether he was referring to his lack of social and networking activities. But when he continued, 'look at his handwriting, tiny letters slanting to the left', I realized that he was just reading the hand-writing rather than what it contained. 'Probably, he has not let his handwriting get the better of him' I blurted out in a lighter vein, with the usual anxiety of a HR man, not wanting to let go off the efforts put in to take the candidate to this stage. 'Why do you say that?' KN asked, as though to ask me what evidence I have got to challenge his assumptions.

The least I wanted at that moment was to say something that could help wipe off any bias about the candidate. Something clicked in my mind and I continued, 'maybe you are right sir, but why not we give the candidate a fair chance? Can we postpone our conclusions till we get enough data and probably start with a null hypothesis- by which we make a conscious assumption that actual is different from what is observed, which might have just been a chance occurrence. What I am trying to say, sir...'

KN cut me short, 'don't start your training class now, you want me to start with a premise that Rakesh fits right for our marketing slot, right? ok, call him'. Something made me feel that the graphology thing was not about the candidate but was more about me. I felt good about myself that I have not become another 'yessir' guy.

You Get What You Expect

What went on during the next half an hour between prez and Rakesh was something commendable. Opening with a casual inquiry about Rakesh's travel from Mumbai set a cordial note and from there, the way the discussions took on to his career-related stuff got Rakesh into a free flow. As he went on, KN's questions seemed as though he wanted to get the best out of Rakesh and Rakesh's responses seemed to be fully in tune with that expectation. During the course of discussions, Rakesh was seen stumbling, for a moment, when he was asked whether he had experience handling large-scale payment defaults and if so, what the lessons learnt were. But KN's cue to his stint in a small business town that faced the brunt during the recession times blew the bulb in Rakesh's head and he was again seen in full form. Towards the close, when Rakesh was asked if he had any questions to ask, he was very candid in saying that it was one of the best interviews he had had and then asked the prez, 'but may I know what is the impression, I am leaving behind?' KN glanced at me and then he said, 'Rakesh, you can take on the baton'. As we wound up, KN endorsed the ief with his comment 'fit'. (You guessed it right; ief is just the good old interview evaluation form).

Self-fulfilling prophecy

There was something in the interview that helped the candidate blossom out. The earlier rounds of interview seemed more like fact-finding mission compared to this round. I could sense one thing: When the person-in-authority creates a positive climate by his inquisitive questioning, interested listening, responsive body language, open gestures etc, the receiving person responds to the expectations. Thus the positive expectations set out positive performance. It can be true the other way round also. If we start with negative expectations, we unconsciously express them through various verbal and non-verbal means and we most often find the candidate coming out poorly conforming to our negative expectations.

A simple truth is *"we get what we expect"*. You must have come across the term *self-fulfilling prophecy*, which means only this: *"we get what we expect"*. "The way managers treat their subordinates is subtly influenced by what they expect of them," said Sterling Livingston in his article, *Pygmalion in Management*, published in the Harvard Business Review (Sept/Oct '88).

The power of positive expectations

It is the expectations of those around us that we more often conform to and similarly those around us rise to the expectations we have about them. If the expectations are positive and encouraging, people tend to surge and perform better and it is also true the other way round too. It is just that people tend to live up to what's expected of them and they tend to do better when treated as if they are capable of success. The way we treat people is subtly influenced by what we expect of them.

We can come up with any number of real-life examples where we evidence this. I have seen this work when I was in school and I am sure this is not any different today. The children who score the top ranks continue to do so and the winning teams continue their winning streak. When we watch the talent shows on TV like the 'Super singer', we are awed by the kind of all-round transformation we see in the children in short span of 3 or 4 months. You will be able to see a discernible difference in the finalists not only in their area of talent like singing, but also in the overall personality. We can see remarkable improvement week-after-week. What do you attribute it to? I don't undermine the tremendous efforts put in by these children. But what motivates that kind of efforts is the recognition of their talents and expectations by those around them, which include their parents, relatives and friends and positive feedback and inputs from the stalwarts in the field who judge their performance and the public recognition.

Pygmalion Effect

A leading researcher on this theme, Robert Rosenthal, labelled this expectancy effect the *"Pygmalion effect"*. The main idea concerning the Pygmalion Effect is that if you believe that someone is capable of achieving greatness, then that person will indeed do so.

Let me give some background of the term Pygmalion, which is drawn from Greek mythology. Pygmalion, the sculptor, fell in love with the statue of a woman he was sculpting and through his sheer power of love, his statue Galatea was aroused to life. Much later, George Barnard Shaw wrote a play, called Pygmalion, in which a professor picks an ordinary flower girl and turns her into a noble lady by his grooming. You may be familiar with the movie *My Fair Lady*, which was inspired by the Shaw's play Pygmalion. So the Pygmalion Effect has come to mean *"you get what you expect."* The main idea concerning The Pygmalion Effect is that if you believe that someone is capable of achieving greatness, then that person will indeed achieve greatness.

Prof Rosenthal's experiment

Professor Rosenthal's research at an elementary school, popularly known as the Oak School experiment, brought out interesting findings on Pygmalion effect. As part of the experiment, the researcher gave the school teachers a list of students' names and told the teachers that these children had scored high marks on a standard IQ Test (known as Harvard Test of Inflected Acquisition), which meant that these particular set of children were expected to show rapid progress in the coming year. None of the children were told about all this. But, the real fact is that the names that researchers gave the teachers were some randomly picked names and they had not put the children to any IQ test. A year later it was found that these randomly-picked children showed significantly greater improvement in their academic performance than did the other children in the group. Prof Rosenthal was surprised by this and came to the conclusion that explained the reason for the remarkable progress these children made. It was just the teachers' expectations from these children and way they treated them out of their expectations. When teachers expected greater intellectual development from certain children, these children did show greater intellectual development. Rosenthal, labelled this expectancy effect the *"Pygmalion effect"*.

Findings of Rosenthal

The Oak School experiment of Rosenthal brought out clearly that the higher expectations of teachers resulted in greater performance of students, which came to be known as Pygmalion effect. Rosenthal listed out four factors that drove the Pygmalion Effect, namely:

1. **Climate factor:** teachers tend to create a warmer climate for those children, both verbally and non-verbally (for example, they will smile more often at them).

2. **Input factor:** teachers will tend to teach more material to children they think are smarter

3. **Response opportunity factor:** children who are expected to bloom academically get more chance to respond.

4. **Feedback factor:** the child gets praised more when she/he is right but gets more differentiated feedback when she/he makes a mistake.

Be a Pygmalion Manager

Can these findings be applied to the world of work and what conclusions can we draw from Rosenthal's work? Obviously, the manager's role is to drive better performance in all and so every manager needs to be aware how the biases or preconceived notions, he holds, can make or mar the performance of his people. Be alert to how you behave towards all team members in terms of the climate you establish, the input you give to each team member, the response you give to each person in terms of support and coaching and how you give differentiated feedback to all.

Four key factors

That Drive Pygmalion effect

1. Climate factor:
- Friendly tone of voice
- Facial expression
- Body language

2. Input factor:
- Assign challenging tasks
- Expand person's skills

3. Response opportunity factor:
- Allow people to express views, ideas and opinions

4. Feedback factor:
- Positive reinforcement
- Constructive criticism

Livingston concludes the article 'Pygmalion in Management' (cited earlier), "If managers are unskilled, they leave scars on the careers of the young people, cut deeply into their self-esteem and distort their image of themselves as human beings. But if they are skillful and have high expectations, subordinates' self-confidence will grow, their capabilities will develop and their productivity will be high. More often than he realizes, the manager is Pygmalion."

Be a Pygmalion Parent

These findings can very well be applied to the world of parenting too. Obviously, as parents, we need to be alert to how we behave towards our children in terms of the climate we establish, the input we give to them, the response and feedback we give that spell out positive expectations and constructive criticism. Pygmalion parent can visibly see their children blossom in self-confidence, develop their capabilities and perform better in studies and their field of pursuit.

When you hold positive expectations about your children, you help them improve their self-concept and their self-esteem. In turn, children believe they are capable of best performance and their performance goes up to meet the level of their own expectations. Your expectations of children and their expectations of themselves are the key factors in how well they perform at studies or any other facet of their talent.

Whether you are a teacher, or a manager or a parent, you can play the Pygmalion to the people in your life as long as your role is to grow people.

REFERENCES AND FURTHER READING

Livingston, J. Sterling, (1988) *Pygmalion in Management,* Harvard Business Review

Rosenthal, R & Jacobson, (1968) *Pygmalion in the Classroom: Teacher Expectations and Pupils' Intellectual Development*, New York: Holt, Rinehart & Winston

Now, Go Beyond and Read

The Pygmalion Manager – *A Perfect Leadership Model for all Times*

By Moid Siddiqui

Thought Note

Who are the people in your life for whom you would like to be a Pygmalion? How would you express your positive expectations about them for making them flourish?

18
Catch Them Right!

*"Outstanding leaders go out of their way to boost the
self-esteem of their personnel. If people believe in
themselves, it's amazing what they can accomplish."*

– Sam Walton

Trust is the Key

I was around fifteen then. Wedding of one of my family friends was
taking place at a place away from my hometown. Since my dad was
preoccupied for some reason, I represented my family at the wedding.
The bridegroom, an incessant smoker, took the liberty of using my shirt
pocket for keeping his cigarette pack. Whenever he wanted to take a
puff, he'd signal to me and sneak away to the backyard. After pulling
out a cigarette, he'd thrust the pack back into my shirt pocket. Though I
was a non-smoker, I didn't mind this for two reasons: one, because none
of my family members was around, I had no qualms about carrying
cigarette pack and two, more importantly, the bogus pride of being
closer to the bridegroom- the hero of the occasion. But as luck would
have it, when we returned after one such jaunt from the backyard, I
saw my dad exchanging pleasantries with his friends. He seemed to be
in a hurry to leave. He must have been looking for me. The moment he
saw me, he came to me asking if I had enough money for the return

fare and very unexpectedly, he pushed a ten rupee note into my shirt pocket. Apparently shocked by what stuck his fingers, he sensed what was inside and left the place without any further word.

I was very upset with myself and mentally prepared myself to explain to him. I thought he'd surely be angry with me and ask me about it, when I returned home. But when we met back at home, he didn't speak a word about that particular incident, leave along reprimanding me. He was talking to me like any other day and he was keenly enquiring about the fitness sessions which I was attending then. Never at any time, did he have any doubt about my indulgence in any smoking or any such habit. Now I am in my fifties and when I recall the incident today, I am still able to see the steadfast trust, my dad had on me. I always cherish my dad as my first mentor.

Managers - Mentors or Tormentors?

I was facilitating a day-long Mentoring workshop for senior managers of a company. One manager asked me at the end of the program, 'Do you think we are not mentoring our subordinates now! What do you expect us to do differently?' I felt all the efforts of the whole day were watered down by this simple question. Actually, the manager who asked me the question was an apt example of 'people don't leave bad companies; but they leave bad bosses' and the management wanted this program primarily to change the negative behaviours of such managers. The old-timers, who learnt their task-oriented style from their task-master bosses, adopted the same style, probably because that was all that they knew when it came to getting things done. It is humorously said, 'when all you have is hammer, all that you see are nails' and they probably saw only nails all around them.

Mentoring- the Ancient Way of Transferring Wisdom

As people grow into leadership levels and take on bigger roles of leading and managing teams, divisions, or business units, one vital responsibility that gets added on, though it may not often be spelt out explicitly in Job Description, is 'mentoring' of the greenhorns. Mentoring is about encouraging people to manage their own learning to develop their skills and performance and support them to explore their potential and become the person they want to be. Mentoring is an effective tool for developing and empowering people. The term "mentor" comes from

Greek mythology where Odysseus entrusts his friend Mentor with the education of his son, similar to the practice of *Gurukul* that was prevalent in ancient India. Though we may not have the same rigour of mentoring today, it is in practice all spheres of life from education to sports to business.

As you move up in your career ladder, it is important that you take on the role of mentor to help people grow in their career. Mentoring calls for an earnest interest to groom the youngsters and it is more about attitude than about skills. One key factor for success as a manager in today's world is your ability to gel well with the younger generation and mentor them into their careers. It is quite a task to provide structured instructions as to what mentors should do on a daily, weekly or monthly basis or to provide mentoring skills to the managers. Any such regimented exercise, devoid of the spirit of mentoring, can be a drain on organisational resources.

Gotcha to Whale Done!

A very simple and essential piece of advice for leaders and potential mentors comes from Ken Blanchard through his book '**Whale Done!**' which is also a catchy phrase the author has coined to term the act of 'catching people doing things right'. Ken brings out beautifully the concepts used by the SeaWorld trainers that turn the killer whales into fascinating creatures doing incredible fetes and how these concepts could apply to the world of human beings.

Generally, as parents or managers, when do we pay attention to people - when they are doing things right, or when they commit some mistakes? Though we know pretty well theoretically that appreciating people can be a great motivator, we can find ourselves or other managers doing quite the opposite thing – catching people wrong. We have seen it in our life that those actions that we give more focus tend to grow and those that we don't wither away. Yet, catching people wrong comes easy for most bosses, whom Ken calls 'seagull' managers – who wait for people to foul up, and then they swoop in, make a lot of noise, and dump on everybody.

Why not try the 'Whale Done' response for a change and see how it works? Start catching people right, praise them immediately for what they did with genuine positive feeling and encourage them to keep up the good work. When you start practising the 'Whale Done' response, you will start wondering how many great motivational opportunities you have lost in the past.

While catching people doing wrong things is a norm among managers, it would be the worst move when it came to training the killer whales. So what do the whale trainers do? They use a technique, which Ken calls as, Redirection Response. Upon encountering any undesirable behaviour on the whales' part, they would quickly refocus their energies elsewhere. It is all about accentuating on the positive and expressing trust and confidence and redirecting the energy when mistakes occur. When I read this, I couldn't help recalling the episode that I have talked about in the beginning of this chapter.

Taking Cue from Yoga Masters

In a similar way Ken draws his valuable lessons in people management from the SeaWorld trainers, I felt there are quite a few things a mentor could learn by observing the way the yoga trainers teach their students to learn some difficult yoga postures or *asanas*.

1. **Drill the habit of 'learning by doing':** You cannot simply learn the difficult postures of yoga just by listening to your yoga master. What masters do is to get you into doing right away. You get to listen to instructions as you practice and now your listening is more intense because it has immediate relevance to what you do.

    Mentoring is not about giving monologues to your captive protégés but getting them into action. Assign them projects and assignments where they can get hands-on experience. Best way to help them is to guide them by sharing from your experience the possible pitfalls they need to be wary of. It is not enough if you have the mastery on the tasks at your disposal, you need to be a good coach to help and support the other people learn the expertise from you.

2. **Give it when they need it the most:** Masters were doing rounds and giving us instructions, but were not intervening into every step. The mere feeling that they were around gave us the confidence to try out postures which we would dare not, left to ourselves. And help was at hand, when we faced difficulty.

It is but natural that a greenhorn would be twice careful about trying out anything new for the fear of making mistakes and would rather avoid the risk. But that doesn't mean that you spoon-feed. As a mentor, all you need to do is to give them the confidence that when you are around, they can't go wrong and if at all they do, you are there to assure '*main hoon na*'.

3. **Push for the little extra stretch:** A maxim we have in our vernacular says, 'what was not bent at five can't be bent at fifty'. After attending the yoga session, I don't subscribe to this view anymore. You can, if you persevere to bend of course, under the guidance of a right coach. Yes, there could be pain in trying to flex what has hardened up for years. But the gentle push the masters gave at the right point made us stretch beyond the normal and the feeling that we were capable of doing it took the pain out of the extra-stretch.

    Mentoring is no different. It is the onus of mentors to ensure that their protégés do not settle into a comfort zone that may mar their growth. Mentors need to give that extra push to stretch them beyond the comfort zone and take them to newer levels consistently.

4. **Support when they tilt:** Sometimes, when a beginner in an organization is assigned to a difficult and challenging project that calls for coping with different pushes and pulls, demanding customers and tight deadlines, they may tend to lose emotional balance and might decide to call it quits.

    All that is needed of you, as a mentor is to provide that emotional support to keep your protégés in balance like our yoga masters do, while coaching pupils on difficult postures. The masters were right there with the learners and provided a kind of scaffolding support to prevent us from tilting and falling off while trying some difficult upside-down postures like *Sirasasana*

5. **Make them feel good even in awkward positions:** A beginner, when trying to do a new thing, could get into awkward situation until s/he learns the ropes and becomes adept at it. You would agree with me if you could recall the time you made your first presentation to top management.

Many a times, awkward situations thwart the youngsters from trying it out again in future and becoming better at it. If it is a crucial skill for success, then it could mar their growth. But as a mentor, you can help a great deal in such situations by elevating their feelings and giving constructive feedback while eradicating the awkward feeling associated with initial failures.

If you have been doing all these already, you have it in you already to be a potential mentor and you don't probably need to sit through a training session to learn all these.

৵৽৵৽৵৽

Now Go Beyond and read

Whale Done! *The Power of Positive Relationships*

By Ken Blanchard et al

Thought Note

Can you spot at least two mentoring opportunities in your daily life during the next one week? How would you make those moments mutually beneficial?

Can you consciously look for 'catching people right' whether at home or in workplace and give a 'whale done' response to them?

19
Breaking the Barriers for Marching Ahead

"The goal is not to be better than the other man,
but your previous self."

- Dalai Lama XIV

'Hi, Can I talk to Bharath' the caller from an unknown number.

'Yes, here'

'I am Andreas, working for a German MNC in Chennai. Do you coach executives?'

Honestly, I have not done any until then. But I didn't want to sound inexperienced and at the same time I also wanted to be true about my lack of coaching experience.

'How did you get my reference?' I asked, as I was thinking on how to take the conversation forward.

'Linkedin' came the crisp reply. I could recall that I had mentioned 'facilitator and coach' in my profile. I deemed coaching to be akin to leadership training, in which I have had more than a decade-long experience. But I knew that did not entail me to call myself an 'executive coach'.

'Oh,' I mumbled and prolonged the talk, 'I have been training people in different behavioural areas and I have informally coached those who seek my help during my training'.

Sensing that the caller was losing patience, I quickly added, 'but honestly, I have not done any formal executive coaching, nor have I got any coaching training or certification'. I thought he would cut the conversation.

'Fine, why not we meet and find out. If I cannot work with you, I will tell it you straight. If you feel so you also tell me so.' That was curt and professional.

I said 'yes.'

And we met the same weekend over a cup of coffee at Hotel Park Hyatt and spent about an hour chatting about things that kept us going and things we looked for in our relationship. The chemistry worked between us and we decided to go ahead with the agreement that anytime we felt things were not going well for any of us, we would stop.

A man of few words, Andreas is straight forward and puts across what he wants without much verbose. He expects the same from others, which comes through in his non-verbals. Starting his career as a Trainee, Andreas has reached a fairly senior level in less than two decades with the company. He has recently been moved to India as operations head, which he finds a totally different assignment compared to his previous tenure in China. From the conversation, I could see his current challenges were two-fold: one, his recent move to India which called for understanding and adjusting to the prevalent work culture, and two: his vertical career growth from a level departmental head – leading a supply chain function- to plant head- heading a team of departmental heads. He was very candid when he said he had to spend a lot of time in meetings, listening to all the nonsense people throw around for making up for their inefficiency.

As I got on with my assignment and first meeting, which of course, was to the mutual satisfaction, the onward course was not clear to me. I could lend him help, when it came to understanding the cultural psycho-dynamics and people. But I was at loss, when it came to making him see his own flaws, which probably could help him become a more effective leader. Though he didn't say in so many words, it was clear that he had difficulty in getting things done and his typical style of giving firm directions and setting tight deadlines were not working anymore. He needed to adapt himself when it came to managing the managers and leading the leaders.

I was wondering how to take up this sensitive conversation with him and bring out his obvious flaws. I casually shared my problem with my friend Rajesh without giving many specifics. Rajesh is a voracious reader and is a go-to person for me at such times. It was not of much help since I felt whatever he suggested was not practicable. But in a couple of days, I received a parcel. Rajesh had flipkarted a book *'What Got You Here Won't Get You There'*. Before even I flipped through the book, I called Rajesh and took a spoof on his gift, 'I am yet to get here; where is the question of my getting there?' Without relishing my humour, he asked me in a serious tone, 'have you started going through?' When I replied with a No, he said, 'please do that first'.

What Got You Here Won't Get You There was a real eye-opener for me, not only on how to tread the sensitive areas of personal flaws with Andreas, but to get an insight into my own flaws and work on them. The next few weeks of my work with Andreas revolved around the themes in the book. We took on the list of **20 habits** that the author points out as transactional flaws that hold us back from getting where we want to be. When we, Andreas and me, started dissecting ourselves – our own behavior on how we rated ourselves on these flaws, the exercise became interesting and created openness about ourselves. Thanks to Marshall, I had no anxiety about my coaching skills anymore with Andreas, as our relationship turned out to be more of friendship than anything else.

Yes, our relationship became primarily one of friendship and the coaching was more mutual – both were learning from each other. I must thank Andreas for making me recognize the unexplored coach in me and Marshall Goldsmith for playing the legendary *Dronacharya* for me to flourish the coach in me, the *Ekalavya*. For those uninitiated into Indian Mythology, *Ekalavya* is a character in the legendary epic *Mahabharata* who by invoking his *Guru Drona's* blessings learnt his archery skills, though he had no any direct contact with Guru. If you are aspiring to be a coach, Marshall has a lot to offer through his books, and his freely-accessible library on the internet (at www.marshallgoldsmithlibrary. com) is a virtual treasure trove.

I borrow heavily from Marshall's book in putting up the rest of the chapter, since I am hard-put to paraphrase without losing the essence of his thoughts. When you dwell into the details of the 20 habits or the leadership challenges, you would be able to identify yourselves with some of them and you may even be surprised to see the exact words you probably sometimes utter. Those are the symptoms to look for to check whether we are afflicted with that particular flaw. Here goes the list of interpersonal challenges enumerated by Marshall:

1. **Winning too much:** The need to win at all costs and in all situations.

2. **Adding too much value:** The overwhelming desire to add our 2 cents to every discussion.

3. **Passing judgment:** The need to rate others and impose our standards on them.

4. **Making destructive comments:** The needless sarcasm and cutting remarks that we think make us witty.

5. **Starting with 'No', 'But', 'However':** The overuse of these negative qualifiers which secretly say to everyone that I'm right and you're wrong.

6. **Telling the world how smart we are:** The need to show people we're smarter than they think we are.

7. **Speaking when angry:** Using emotional volatility as a management tool.

8. **Negativity, or "Let me explain why that won't work":** The need to share our negative thoughts even when we weren't asked.

9. **Withholding information:** The refusal to share information in order to maintain an advantage over others.

10. **Failing to give proper recognition:** The inability to give praise and reward.

11. **Claiming credit that that we don't deserve:** The most annoying way to overestimate our contribution to any success.

12. **Making excuses:** The need to reposition our annoying behavior as a permanent fixture so people excuse us for it.

13. **Clinging to the past:** The need to deflect blame away from ourselves and onto events and people from our past; a subset of blaming everyone else.

14. **Playing favorites:** Failing to see that we are treating someone unfairly.

15. **Refusing to express regret:** The inability to take responsibility for our actions, admit we're wrong, or recognize how our actions affect others.

16. **Not listening:** The most passive-aggressive form of disrespect for colleagues.

17. **Failing to express gratitude:** The most basic form of bad manners.

18. **Punishing the messenger:** The misguided need to attack the innocent who are usually only trying to help us.

19. **Passing the buck:** The need to blame everyone but ourselves.

20. **An excessive need to be "me":** Exalting our faults as virtues simply because they're who we are.

How We Can Change For the Better

Marshall provides us with a seven step method for overcoming the above habits and bettering our interpersonal relationships.

Feedback: Never respond to feedback by arguing about it. Instead, write it down and consider it later when your immediate flared up emotions have become calmer. Thank the person for offering feedback, put the advice aside for a while, and then look at it later with a cool head, and you'll often find something specific, you can improve on. If you want to be proactive about feedback, don't be afraid to ask for it, but never argue about it.

Apologising: Apologise, if you realize that you have done something wrong, either recently or in the past. Swallow a bit of pride, go up to the person, and just apologize for whatever it is. Likely, you'll both feel better for it - you'll lose at least some of the bad feeling and the other person will feel better too.

Telling the world, or advertising: Apologies don't mean anything if you are not effecting the changes in you that warranted the apology in the first place. So, you need to define the changes you're going to make and to let everyone know about them, especially the people you've apologized to.

Listening: Listen to people, when they are speaking to you. Don't interrupt them, and try to fully understand what they're saying before framing your response. This is always a strong tactic to use when someone is trying to talk to you. If you can't fully describe and articulate the message someone is trying to deliver to you, your response is guaranteed to be less accurate and thorough than it could be if you listened to the message and to the messenger.

Thanking: Just make sure that you thank everyone who contributes to your success, both directly and in public opportunities when given the chance.

Following up: Once you have identified your bad habits, you need to work on eliminating them and also have a regular follow-up to prevent their recurrence. Check with the people to whom you have apologised if you are doing well on the commitments you have made. Stay diligent yourself, and try to remind yourself often of your goals.

Practicing "feedforward": When you are already on track in eliminating your negative habits, go forward. Now, ask for some suggestions on where you should go with these changes. Ask someone who you've had experience with in the past for one or two specific things that you can do in the future to help with the behaviours you're working on. Don't just stop at asking, but listen, thank them, then work on implementing them. While the feedback is about the past, "feedforward" is about the future.

Pulling Out the Stops

How do you apply the rules of change?

Be transparent on your expectations from your subordinates; be very clear to them on what's expected of them specifically. Similarly, seek clarity from your boss of his/her expectations from you; be sure to ask the specifics. If you spot any of the twenty flaws popping up in your workplace, be candid about it with that person, but don't allow it degenerate into whispers and backstabbing.

In essence, a healthy organization is one that is open to looking at its problems and weeds them out immediately. Most of the major concerns are mostly the minor issues that were not dealt with right in the beginning. If they are detected early and the root causes are quickly addressed with candour and honesty, then many of the later crises can be averted.

"If you want to change anything about yourself, the best time to start is *now*. Ask yourself, 'what am I willing to change now?' Just do that" exhorts Marshall.

So, if you choose to walk with Marshall, 'getting there' is not far away.

ళ్ళళ్ళళ్ళ

Now, go beyond and read

What Got You Here Won't Get You There

By Marshall Goldsmith

Thought Note

Which are the top two or three of the inter-personal challenges or habitual flaws (from the list of 20), you feel you need to work on?

What actions you want to take for overcoming them?

Going Beyond...

The joy of reading is multiplied when we share the joy with others. And what is even more fulfilling is when the person, to whom you suggested something out of your experience comes back and tells you that it worked well for them too. I have written this with the conviction that some of the thoughts expressed here could help you in going beyond the bounds of self-doubts and limitations and pave way for discovering yourself in new light. Or maybe, you are already well ahead on the path, the book came in just as a one more reinforcement for the thoughts you already strongly hold. Or perhaps, there are things that you don't agree with or things that you feel don't still work the way they are said to. Whatever be it, I would be keen to know from you. If you feel like telling me, you may do so at connectBYB@gmail.com and I would be too happy to interact with you and learn.

It is an irreversible journey we are on. After each reading, you are not the same person. Like they say you cannot visit the same place twice, you cannot read the same book twice, because you –something in you- has already changed after your first reading. After all, we are nothing but a heap of impressions we carry along the journey. Let's keep going beyond us- the we we are now.

It is in the listening of the audience lies the power of the speaker. It is in the openness of the readers, the writers thrive. As I sign off, I acknowledge you for coming along with me and letting me go on uninterrupted and thereby, bestowing upon me the greatest freedom, a writer can ever yearn for: the freedom to be myself and to express myself.

Be You! Be Amazing!
Bharath Gopalan

Some More of My Bests

If I were to go on this saga of sharing the experience of reading, there are many more books that I consider as essential part of my thought journey and I am sharing with you my list of such books, in a random order, in this section. As you browse the list, you may be reminded of the books you had lent to someone and never got back or the books you borrowed from someone, that have almost permanently adorned your book shelves. I say this, because, when I made the list of books, I could see how some titles/ books were so tied with the memories of some people- those who lent to me or borrowed from me. It gave me an opportunity to remember them with gratitude.

1. Living At The Source by Vivekananda
2. As A Man Thinketh by James Allen
3. The Fifth Discipline by Peter Senge
4. Turning Point by APJ Abdul Kalam
5. Put Your Dreams to Test by John Maxwell
6. How to Be Interesting by Edward de Bono
7. Bringing Out The Best In People by Aubrey C Daniel
8. Think Like A Winner by Walter Doyle Staples
9. Principle Centered Leadership by Stephen R Covey
10. The Road Less Travelled by M Scott Peck
11. Future Shock by Alvin Toffler
12. The Unschooled Mind by Howard Gardner
13. Life Ahead by J Krishnamurthy
14. Notes To Myself Hugh Prather
15. All I really Need To Know I Learned in Kindergarten by Robert Fulghum
16. The Seven Spiritual Laws of Success by Deepak Chopra
17. Re-Imagine by Tom Peters

18. Leading the Revolution by Gary Hamel
19. Purple Cow by Seth Godin
20. Influence by Robert Ciadini
21. Getting Things Done by David Allen
22. The Complete Mental Fitness Book by Tom Wujec
23. Good To Great by Jim Collins
24. Steps To The Top by Zig Zigglar
25. The Platinum Rule by Dr Tony Alessandra et al
26. The Silva Mind Control Method by Jose Silva
27. The Art of Japanese Management by Richard Tanner Pascale and Anthony G.Athos
28. The One Minute Millionaire by Mark Victor Hansen and Robert Allen
29. Are You Smart Enough To Work At Google by William Poundstone
30. The Manager's Book of Checklists by Derek Rowntree
31. On Becoming A Person by Carl Rogers
32. On Becoming A Leader by Warren Bennis
33. The Creative Problem Solver's Toolbox by Richard Fobes
34. The Art of Speeches and Presentations by Philip Collins
35. Connect The Dots by Rashmi Bansal
36. Tactics – The Art & Science of Success by Edward de Bono
37. The Mindmap Book by Tony Buzan
38. Contagious Optimism by David Mezzapelle
39. What to Say When You Talk To Yourself by Shad Helmstetter
40. The Power of Now by Eckhart Tolle
41. Pulling Your own Strings by Dr Wayne W Dyer
42. The Decision Book by Mikael Krogerus and Roman Tschappeler
43. How to Sell Yourself by Joe Girard
44. Exercising Influence by B. Kim Barnes
45. The Language of Success by Tom Sant

46. The Science of Mind by Ernest S Holmes
47. Failing Forward John C Maxwell
48. The Plateau Effect by Bob Sullivan and Hugh Thompson
49. Anatomy of an Illness by Norman Cousins
50. The Last Lecture by Randy Pausch
51. You can win by Shiv Khera